The Full Ride Scholarships Book: Attend College Debt-free by Chrisnuel Publishing.

Published by Chrisnuel publishing.

Distributed by Amazon LLC.

Copyright © 2022 by Chrisnuel Publishing.

All rights reserved. No part of this book may be reproduced, stored in a retrieval system, or transmitted, in any form or by any means, electronic, mechanical, photocopying, recording, or otherwise, without the written permission of Chrisnuel Publishing. This book is protected under International Copyright Conventions.

Trademarks: Chrisnuel does not claim ownership of the on/around campus images used in the book as well as the organizational logos registered trademarks or trade names of their respective holders.

They were all used with the sole purpose of profiling the institutions of which they describe. Furthermore, images were used following the fair use guidelines in regards to the scholarship and academic setting for which this book is exactly created for. The book was carefully crafted out for the good of the general public.

Credits: Quality research was done during the production of this book. We wish to acknowledge some highly helpful platforms from which accurate data was sourced – US news (*college data*), Educationdata.org (*student loan data*), and Wikipedia (*general inquiries*). Also credits to Convertful for the abstract illustration used on the book cover.

Disclaimer: The information listed in this book was curated to help students get a degree without having to owe thousands of dollars in student loan. The author and publisher have done proper research and put in their best efforts in this book. We are not in affiliation with any university/college listed in this book. Also, this book is not endorsed by any school or organization listed in it.

Although the best resources and research was put into the production of this book, it is sold with the understanding that neither the publisher nor the authors are engaged in rendering legal, accounting or other professional services. If legal advice or other expert assistance is required, the services of a competent professional person should be sought. Therefore, Chrisnuel specifically disclaim any responsibility for any liability, loss or risk, personal or otherwise, which is incurred as a consequence, directly or indirectly, of the use and application of any of the contents of this book.

This publication is designed to provide quality and authoritative information in regards to the subject matter covered here. However, the authors make no warranties in regards to the totality of the contents of the book and specifically disclaim any implied warranties or merchantability or fitness for a particular purpose. Therefore, the information, details, and opinions listed in here are not guaranteed to produce any particular results.

Printed and bound in the United States of America.

Table of Contents

Introduction 1
   The Student Loan Debt Problem 2
   Definition of Full Ride Scholarship 2
   Types of Full Ride Scholarships 3
   Scholarships Renewal 8

Chapter 1
Full Ride Institutional Scholarships 9
(Full Ride Scholarships offered by Colleges/Universities)

   Alabama to Georgia .... 9 – 32
   Hawaii to Maryland .... 33 – 56
   Massachusetts to New Jersey .... 57 – 75
   New Mexico to South Carolina .... 76 – 109
   South Dakota to Wyoming .... 110 – 137
(All States are Listed | Scholarships are Arranged by States)

Chapter 2
Full Ride External Scholarships 138
(Full Ride Scholarships from organizations, individuals, companies, etc.)

Chapter 3
Need Based Scholarships

– Ivy League & Top Colleges 202

Chapter 4
Scholarship Application Tips 215
   Scholarship Golden Rules 215
   Scholarship Process Flowchart 216

Chapter 5
Definition of Key Terms 217
   FAFSA | National Merit | etc. 217

End Notes 219

Dedication

This book is dedicated to Almighty God and to all scholars – both U.S. and International scholars – who wish to attend college on a full ride scholarship and graduate debt-free.

May Your Wishes Come True !

A Sample View of Scholarships Listed.

Read Through To See "All The Scholarships" Listed in This Book
(Listings are State by State — From Alabama down to Wyoming)

ALABAMA

Alabama State University

Location: Montgomery, Alabama
Setting: Urban (172 Acres)
Undergraduate Enrollment: 3,614
Type: Public

Presidential Academic Scholarship: Full tuition, books, required fees, on-campus room & board for four years of undergraduate study.

Requirements: ACT Score of 26 or SAT score of 1240-1270 | High school GPA of 3.76

Academic Excellence Scholarsip: Full tuition, books and required fees.

Requirements: ACT Score of 22 or SAT score of 1240-1270 | High school GPA of 3.51-3.75

Application Deadline: February 15

Application link: https://www.alasu.edu/admissions/undergrad-admissions/asu-academic-scholarships

Alabama A&M University

Location: Huntsville, Alabama
Setting: Urban (1,173 Acres)
Undergraduate Enrollment: 5,093
Type: Public

AAMU Presidential Scholarship: Full tuition, room, board, fees and $1000 book allowance per semester.

Requirements: High School GPA of 3.75 or above | Act Score of 28 or above/ Sat score of 1310 or above | Citizen or legal resident of United States.

Application Deadline: January 15

Application link: https://www.aamu.edu/admissions-aid/financial-aid/scholarships/

Introduction

A four-year degree will cost anywhere from **$100,000 to $350,000,** depending on the choice of institution.

It is no news that the "problem of college-loan debt" is increasingly becoming a problem for most American adults. In the consumer debt category, student loan debt is ranked No. 2 only surpassed by mortgages. Student loan debt in the United States totals **$1.748 trillion.** The outstanding federal loan balance is **$1.620 trillion** and accounts for 92.7% of all student loan debt.

The reason why college education is so expensive circles around many factors which include, but are not limited to the growing demand for college degrees, lower government funding, pricey student amenity packages, and skyrocketing costs of administrators, amongst other factors.

Well, because of these, many students are left with no choice but to borrow student loans to attend college.

Let's take a look at some student loan debt statistics:

- In a single year, **31.8%** of undergraduate students accepted federal loans (note, a large number of students also take private loans).
- Public university attendees borrow an average of **$32,880** to attain a bachelor's degree.
- Private, non-profit university attendees borrow **$35,983,** and private or-profit university students borrow **$42,551**.

These are average numbers meaning that more than half of student loan borrowers collect far more than the amounts listed above.

Although student loans has their meager benefits, the disadvantages tend to overweigh their advantages in most cases.

Loans accrue interest over time. They force borrowers to postpone further life goals in order to repay them. It is virtually impossible to get off student loans if the borrower cannot pay them back. Moreover, failing to repay your loan could ruin your credit score coupled with the uneasiness that comes with remembering the loan repayment.

The Good News . . . . .

The good news is that all these can be avoided. A great way to escape is to get a Full Ride Scholarship. Find out more in the sections below!

──────────── *Data Source -- educationdata.org/student-loan-debt-statistics*

Introduction

What is a Full Ride Scholarship?

A full ride scholarship is a financial award that covers all of a student's college expenses. A typical full ride scholarship covers full tuition, fees, books, room & board – some even extend to providing monthly stipends, research stipends, travel abroad funds, laptops, etc.

The best part is that it doesn't have to be repaid.

Both "Full Ride" and "Full-Ride" are correct and can be used. We will be using "Full Ride Scholarship" in this book for uniformity.

Types of Full Ride Scholarships Awarded

A full ride scholarship can be awarded based on different factors – which include, but are not limited to the following: Full Ride Academic Scholarships, Full Ride Military Scholarships, Full Ride Athletic Scholarships, Full Ride Leadership/Extracurricular Scholarships, Need-Based Full Ride Scholarships, Private/Government Sponsored Full Ride Scholarships.

Introduction

The simple truth about full ride scholarships is that students who aim to get them need to exhibit high excellence either in academics, sports, or extracurricular activities like having good leadership potential.

The most common type of full ride scholarship available in large numbers across a variety of schools across the United States of America is the Academic Full Ride Scholarship(s). These are awarded based on excellent academic performance typically to the top applicant(s) pool. Of course, something goes for something, here the scholar has to exhibit excellence in their studies (GPA, Test scores, etc.) to receive a full ride scholarship.

Let's take an in-depth look at each of the instances where you can receive a full ride scholarship:

1) Full Ride Academic Scholarships
2) Full Ride Military Scholarships
3) Full Ride Athletic Scholarships
4) Full Ride Leadership/Extracurricular Scholarships
5) Need-Based Full Ride Scholarships
6) Private/Government Sponsored Full Ride Scholarships

Introduction

1) Full Ride Academic Scholarships

These are the most popular type of full ride scholarships. They are awarded to students who have great academic records – strong GPAs, high test scores (SAT, ACT, CLT), and/or AP/honors classes.

They go hand in hand with superb extracurricular activities like leadership, volunteering, and community involvement. You can get this type of scholarship when applying for admissions at a college/university that offers them.

There are hundreds of full ride academic scholarships at various institutions listed in this book. Send in your application to as many as possible where you are qualified.

Thousands of individual full ride scholarships are available at universities across the United States of America.

Introduction

2) Full Ride Military Scholarships

The United States Army, Air force, and Navy offer full ride scholarships through their ROTC scholarship programs. ROTC stands for Reserve Officers' Training Corps – it is a college-to-military program that trains students to become commissioned officers while also earning their academic degrees.

After graduation, ROTC recipients are immediately employed and are drafted into the military to serve for an obligatory 8 years.

The program is offered at more than 1,700 colleges and universities across the United States.

ROTC programs offer two-, three-, and four-year scholarships based on the amount of time remaining in the applicant(s) studies. Most ROTC scholarships completely pay for college expenses, including tuition, room and board, monthly stipends, and course materials.

Scholars in ROTC are eligible to apply for partial and full ride scholarships, but enrolling in ROTC does not guarantee a scholarship. ROTC scholarships can be competitive, and they often demand academic excellence as a condition for receiving award money, along with the eight-year commitment to military service.

ROTC Scholarships are usually competitive and have strict standards.

Detailed information on the various ROTC scholarships are listed in this book.

Introduction

3) Full Ride Leadership/Extracurricular Scholarships

These types of scholarships usually go hand in hand with full ride academic scholarships. Active participation in leadership, volunteering, or other extracurricular activities are usually listed as secondary criteria for such full ride scholarships.

Those extracurricular activity scholarships tend to focus more on the extracurricular requirements, but require satisfactory academic performances.

4) Private/Government Sponsored Full Ride Scholarships

These are full ride scholarships that are sponsored either by the government, foundations, companies, or individuals. Some of this type of scholarships can be used at any school of your choice, while some can be used only at specific schools. The same scenario applies to the major requirements – some allow you to choose any major of choice while some are restricted to particular majors. An example of a government-sponsored full ride scholarship is the USDA/1890 National scholars program which allows recipients to pursue only majors in agriculture and related disciplines. An example of a foundation scholarship is "The Gates Scholarship" which gives full ride scholarships to any college to study any major of your choice.

Introduction

5) Full Ride Athletic Scholarships

Full ride athletic scholarships are awarded to students with very good athletics abilities. They can be found at some point(s) in this book.

6) Full Ride Need-based Scholarships

These are scholarships awarded to indigent, but bright students. They cover the full cost of attendance to students who have financial need; and demonstrate excellence in academics or any other areas the scholarship program deems fit.

This type of scholarship is very common at Ivy League and top colleges in the US. They can be awarded by colleges, individuals, or organizations. These scholarships extend generosity to even excellent international students.

Superb academic performance, athletics prowess, special talents, specific nativity are some of the traits than usually earn students full ride need-based scholarships. There is a section dedicated to full-ride need-based scholarships listed in this book.

Explore and find out how you can win a scholarship award!

Introduction

Scholarships Renewal

Scholars who are privileged to receive a full ride scholarship must however note that certain renewal requirements need to be met to retain the scholarship award. The journey does not just end in the initial earning of the award, the scholar(s) has to keep on exuding the excellence that earned them the scholarship at first.

The renewal requirements for the respective full ride scholarships vary, therefore the scholar should ensure that the renewal requirement(s) for the full ride award they have received are duly met.

We wish you every success in getting a full ride scholarship and making the most of it.

✍ **Note: For Paperback readers, pages will appear in black & white. For eBook readers, pages will appear in color.**

CHAPTER 1

FULL RIDE INSTITUTIONAL $CHOLARSHIP$

ALABAMA

1. Alabama A&M University

Location: Huntsville, Alabama
Setting: Urban (1,173 Acres)
Undergraduate Enrollment: 5,093
Type: Public

AAMU Presidential Scholarship: Full tuition, room, board, fees and $1000 book allowance per semester.

Requirements: High School GPA of 3.75 or above | Act Score of 28 or above/ Sat score of 1310 or above | Citizen or legal resident of United States.

Application Deadline: January 15

Application link: https://www.aamu.edu/admissions-aid/financial-aid/scholarships/

2. University of Alabama at Huntsville

Location: Huntsville, Alabama
Setting: City (432 Acres)
Undergraduate Enrollment: 8,027
Type: Public

Platinum Award of Academic Distinction:

Full tuition, room, board, and course fee stipend (up to $1000).

Requirements: National Merit Finalists, National Achievement Finalists, National Hispanic Recognition Program Scholars.

Application Deadline: December 15

Application link: https://www.uah.edu/admissions/undergraduate/financial-aid/scholarships/freshmen

Join Our Mailing List Here: https://bit.ly/chrisnuel-publishing

ALABAMA

3. University of Montevallo

Location: Montevallo, Alabama
Setting: Rural (160 Acres)
Undergraduate Enrollment: 2,228
Type: Public

Montevallo Ambassador Scholarship: Full tuition, fees, room and board.

Requirements: High School GPA of 3.5 or above | ACT Score of 30 or above / SAT score of 1360 or above

Application Deadline: January 15

Application link: https://www.montevallo.edu/admissions-aid/undergraduate-admissions/scholarships/entering-freshmen-academic/

4. Troy University

Location: Troy, Alabama
Setting: Rural (1,836 Acres)
Undergraduate Enrollment: 12,712
Type: Public

The Scholars Award: Full tuition, room and board.

Requirements: 30-36 ACT, 1360-1600 SAT | 3.7 GPA

Application Deadline: Check site for more details.

Application link: https://www.troy.edu/scholarships-costs-aid/scholarships/undergraduate-scholarships.html

ALABAMA

5 Alabama State University

Location: Montgomery, Alabama
Setting: Urban (172 Acres)
Undergraduate Enrollment: 3,614
Type: Public

Presidential Academic Scholarship: Full tuition, books, required fees, on-campus room & board for four years of undergraduate study.

Requirements: ACT Score of 26 or SAT score of 1240-1270 | High school GPA of 3.76

Academic Excellence Scholarship: Full tuition, books and required fees.

Requirements: ACT Score of 22 or SAT score of 1240-1270 | High school GPA of 3.51-3.75

Application Deadline: February 15

Application link: https://www.alasu.edu/admissions/undergrad-admissions/asu-academic-scholarships

6 University of Alabama at Tuscaloosa

Location: Tuscaloosa, Alabama
Setting: Suburban (1,143 Acres)
Undergraduate Enrollment: 31,670
Type: Public

National Merit Finalist: Full tuition, four years on-campus room, $3,500 stipend per year, $2000 study abroad stipend, $2000 book scholarship.

Requirements: ACT Score of 32 or SAT score of 1420 | High school GPA of 3.8

Academic Elite Scholarship: Full tuition, one year on-campus room, $8,500 stipend per year, $2000 book scholarship + plus more

Requirements: ACT Score of 32 or SAT score of 1420 | High school GPA of 3.8

Application Deadline: December 15

Application link: https://scholarships.ua.edu/

ALABAMA

7. Tuskegee University

Location: Tuskegee, Alabama
Setting: Rural (5,000 Acres)
Undergraduate Enrollment: 2,280
Type: Private

Distinguished Presidential Scholarship: Full tuition, room, board, and $800 book allowance

Requirements: High School GPA of 3.7 or above | SAT score of 1390 or ACT equivalent.

Application Deadline: May 1

Application link: https://www.tuskegee.edu/programs-courses/scholarships/freshman-scholarships

8. Faulkner University

Location: Montgomery, Alabama
Setting: Suburban (84 Acres)
Undergraduate Enrollment: 2,192
Type: Private

National Merit Finalist: Full tuition, room, board, and mandatory fees.

Requirements: National Merit Finalists.

Application Deadline: March 2

Application link: https://www.faulkner.edu/admissions/scholarships/

ARKANSAS

1. University of Arkansas at Little Rock

Location: Little Rock, Arkansas
Setting: Urban (250 Acres)
Undergraduate Enrollment: 7,006
Type: Public

Donaghey Scholars Program: Full tuition, fees, $6,000-$10,000 yearly stipend, study abroad funding, laptop, housing subsidy, up to four year Awarded.

Requirements: Average GPA usually is 3.9 | Average Act Score usually is 30 | US citizens or permanent residents. There are other scholarships available for out-of-state students.

Application Deadline: February 1

Application link: https://ualr.edu/scholarships/freshmen/

2. Harding University

Location: Searcy, Arkansas
Setting: Subruban (350 Acres)
Undergraduate Enrollment: 3,574
Type: Private

National Merit Scholarship: Full tuition, standard room & board, technology fee.

Requirements: National Merit Finalist.

Application Deadline: Check site for more details.

There are scholarships available for International Students.

Application link: https://www.harding.edu/admissions/scholarships

3. Philander Smith College

Location: Little Rock, Arkansas
Setting: Urban (9 Acres)
Undergraduate Enrollment: 799
Type: Private

Presidential Scholarship: Full tuition, fees, books, room & board.

Requirements: High School GPA of 3.4 or above | SAT score of 1200+ or 25+ ACT equivalent

Application Deadline: March 1

Application link: https://www.philander.edu/admissions/paying-for-college/scholarships

ARKANSAS

4. Hendrix College

Location: Conway, Arkansa
Setting: Subruban (175 Acres)
Undergraduate Enrollment: 1,066
Type: Private

President's & Madison Murphy Scholarship: Full tuition, board, half the room.

Requirements: ACT Score of 32 or SAT score of 1430 | High school GPA of 3.6

Hays Memorial Scholarship: Full tuition, fees, room, board.

Requirements: ACT Score of 32 or SAT score of 1430 | High school GPA of 3.6

Application Deadline: November 15

Application links:
https://www.hendrix.edu/financialaid/scholarships/

5. University of Arkansas at Pine Bluff

Location: Pine Bluff, Arkansas
Setting: City (318 Acres)
Undergraduate Enrollment: 2,507
Type: Public

UAPB ARMY ROTC Scholarship: Full tuition, fees, room and board, books and up to $16,000 allowances.

Requirements: U.S. citizen | Cumulative GPA of 2.5; ACT score of 19 | Pass the Army physical fitness test.

Application Deadline: Check site for more details.

Application link:
https://www.uapb.edu/academics/military_science/scholarships.aspx

ARIZONA

1 Grand Canyon

Location: Phoenix, Arizona
Setting: Urban (100 Acres)
Undergraduate Enrollment: 58,997
Type: Private

ROTC Scholarships: Full tuition, the option of room and board in place of tuition, additional allowances for books and fees, monthly living allowances for each school year, worth up to $500.

Application Deadline: Check site for more details.

Application link: https://www.gcu.edu/financial-aid/scholarships-grants#h-rotc-scholarships

---

Students Inspiring Students: Full tuition and fees per academic year, except for room and meal charges. Renewable for up to 8 semesters.

Additional Information: Students who receive this scholarship are required to complete 50 hours per semester in the GCU Learning Lounge.

Application link: https://www.gcu.edu/financial-aid/scholarships-grants/additional

CALIFORNIA

1. California State University – Long Beach

Location: Long Beach, California
Setting: Urban (322 Acres)
Undergraduate Enrollment: 33,919
Type: Public

President's Scholarship: Full tuition, campus housing allowance, and subsidies for textbooks, internship, travel abroad, plus more.

Requirements: Top Applicants

Application Deadline: November 1

Application link: https://www.csulb.edu/student-affairs/financial-aid-and-scholarships-office/prospective-students

2. California Institute of Technology

Location: Pasadena, California
Setting: Suburban (124 Acres)
Undergraduate Enrollment: 901
Type: Private

The majority of financial aid awarded to Caltech undergraduates comes from grants. They are all need-based, as the institute does not have a merit aid program. Undergraduate students who fill out a financial aid application will be automatically considered.

Please refer to this site for more details…

https://www.finaid.caltech.edu/TypesofAid/grants#

CALIFORNIA

University of Southern California

Location: Los Angeles, Carlifornia
Setting: Urban (226 Acres)
Undergraduate Enrollment: 19,606
Type: Private

Mork Family Scholarship: Full tuition, $5,000 Housing stipend per year.

Eligibility: Application is open to incoming freshmen through the USC Office of Admission. Candidates are selected from an extremely competitive pool.

There are scholarships available for International students.

Application Deadline: December 1

Application link: https://ahf.usc.edu/meritscholars/merit-scholarships/mork/#morkel

Soka University

Location: Aliso Viejo, Carlifornia
Setting: Suburban (103 Acres)
Undergraduate Enrollment: 392
Type: Private

Soka's Global Merit Scholarship: Covers the entire cost of attendance, full tuition, room and board, travel, personal expenses, books, and supplies.

Soka's Makiguchi scholarship: Covers the entire cost of attendance, full tuition, room and board, travel, personal expenses, books, and supplies.

Soka's Ikeda Scholarship: The most Prestigious Scholarship at Soka University. Covers the entire cost of attendance, full tuition, room and board, travel, personal expenses, books, and supplies.

N.B: Awarded for the duration of one academic year.

Eligibility: This is determined by the dean of enrollment services based on your admissions application. All admitted students are given equal consideration for this award.

Application Deadline: January 15

Application link: https://www.soka.edu/financial-aid-tuition/aid-undergraduate-students/undergraduate-types-aid

COLORADO

1. Colorado State University

Location: Fort Collins, Colorado
Setting: City (4773 Acres)
Undergraduate Enrollment: 25,186
Type: Public

Monfort Scholars Scholarship: Full tuition, fees, books, room & board.

Requirements: Upper 5% of graduating class [#1 or #2 if class is fewer than 40], evidence of scholastic ability, leadership etc., 1300 or higher on SAT(or ACT Equivalent)

Application Deadline: February 1
Application link:
https://financialaid.colostate.edu/scholarships-for-incoming-colorado-resident-freshman/

2. Colorado College

Location: Colorado Springs, Colorado
Setting: City (100 Acres)
Undergraduate Enrollment: 2,025
Type: Private

El Pomar Scholarship: Full tuition and fees, room & board and meal Plan.

Requirements: Coloroda Resident, High school senior, top applicants, eligible for need-based financial aid.

Application Deadline: November 1
Application link:
https://www.coloradocollege.edu/admission/financialaid/scholarships/index.html

CONNECTICUT

1. University of Connecticut

Location: Storrs, Connecticut
Setting: Rural (4,052 Acres)
Undergraduate Enrollment: 18,847
Type: Public

Nutmeg Scholarship: Full Scholarship (Includes direct and Indirect cost of attendance)

Requirements: Connecticut Resident | All Semifinalist/Finalist in the National Hispanic Recognition program or the National Merit competition semifanlists are eligible for nomination | Nominations are made by the Guidance Counselor's office at each Connecticut secondary school.

Day of Pride Scholarship: Full Scholarship (Includes direct and Indirect cost of attendance). Awarded to outstanding Connecticut secondary school seniors from disadvantaged backgrounds.

Requirements: Nominations are made by the Guidance Counselor's office at each Connecticut secondary school | Connecticut Resident.

Stamps Scholars Award: Full support scholarship(tuition, room and board, fees, books, transportation, miscellaneous. Funding for enrichment experiences (up to $12,000 per student)

Requirements: Connecticut Resident | Must qualify for the Nutmeg or Day of pride scholarship.

Application Deadline: October 25

Application link: https://admissions.uconn.edu/cost-aid/scholarship/

2. Western Connecticut State University

Location: Danbury, Connecticut
Setting: Urban (398 Acres)
Undergraduate Enrollment: 4,641
Type: Public

President-to-President Scholarship: In-state tuition and fees for 2 years.

Requirements: Awarded to an outstanding graduating Naugatuck Valley Community College student who has been accepted to WSCU | A minimum 3.3 GPA.

Application Deadline: March 1

Application link: https://www.wcsu.edu/waterbury/scholarship/

DELAWARE

1. University of Delaware

Location: Newark, Delaware
Setting: Suburban (1,996 Acres)
Undergraduate Enrollment: 18,420
Type: Private-Public

ROTC Scholarships

U.S. Air Force ROTC: There are three different types of scholarships under this category.

Please refer to this site for more details…

https://www.afrotc.com/scholarships/

This award covers full tuition and authorized fees, plus a monthly living expense stipend and an annual book stipend.

Requirements: U.S. citizens | SAT composite score of 1240 or ACT composite score of 26 | A minimum cumulative unweighted GPA of 3.0 | Applicant must be physically fit.

Application Deadline: January 14

Application link:
https://www.udel.edu/students/student-financial-services/undergraduate/#

2. Delaware State University

Location: Dover, Delaware
Setting: Suburban (400 Acres)
Undergraduate Enrollment: 4,131
Type: Public

Full Scholarship: Full tuition, fees, room and board, text books and school materials.

This scholarship is available to both in-state and out-of-state students.

Eligibility: U.S. citizens | This scholarship is awarded by the office of admissions to entering full-time, first-year freshmen.

Application Deadline: March 15

Application link:
https://www.desu.edu/admissions/tuition-financial-aid/scholarships

FLORIDA

1. University of West Florida

Location: Penascola, Florida
Setting: Suburban (1,600 Acres)
Undergraduate Enrollment: 9,571
Type: Public

Pace Presidential Scholarship: Full tuition, mandatory fees, a meal plan, on-campus housing, a $600 per-semester textbook stipend, and a one time paid summer research or study abroad experience valued up to $1,500

Requirements: Students are automatically considered for invitation once they are offered admission.

Application Deadline: January 15

Application link:
https://uwf.edu/admissions/undergraduate/cost-and-financial-aid/awards-and-scholarships/presidents-scholarship-competition/

2. Bethune-Cookman University

Location: Daytona Beach, Florida
Setting: Urban (82 Acres)
Undergraduate Enrollment: 2,746
Type: Private

Presidential Scholarship: Full tuition, room, board, and $500 per semester book Scholarship.

Requirements: SAT 1240 OR ACT Composite 26 | 3.75 GPA | Must be a Resident on Campus | Enrollment Fee (Non-Refundable)

Application Deadline: March 1

Application link:
https://www.cookman.edu/admissions/Presidential.html

3. Lynn University

Location: Boca Raton, Florida
Setting: Suburban (123 Acres)
Undergraduate Enrollment: 2,459
Type: Private

Presidential Scholarship: Full tuition, room and board.

Eligibility: 3.65 or higher (on a 4.0 Scale) if test scores were not considered by admission | 3.50 or higher (on a 4.0 Scale) if test score were considered for admission. A minimum SAT score of 1050 or ACT score of 20 is required.

Application Deadline: February 1

Application link:
https://www.lynn.edu/admission/tuition-aid/financial-aid/presidential-scholarship

FLORIDA

4 University of Florida

Location: Gainesville, Florida
Setting: Suburban (2,000 Acres)
Undergraduate Enrollment: 34,931
Type: Public

Machen Florida Opportunity Scholars Program: Awards full grant and scholarship financial aid package to ensure students thrive at UF.

Requirements: Florida Residents | Neither parent may have earned a bachelor's degree | Total family income is less than $40,000 and total family assets, other than home, are less than $25,000.

Application Deadline: October 1

Application link: https://www.sfa.ufl.edu/types-of-aid/scholarships/

5 Barry University

Location: Miami Shores, Florida
Setting: Urban (124 Acres)
Undergraduate Enrollment: 3,523
Type: Private

Stamps Scholars Program: Full tuition, room and board, books, and travel over four years, plus additional $6,000 award for study abroad or other extraordinary learning experience.

Requirements: 3.5 GPA or higher (International equivalent accepted)

Open to U.S and International Freshmen.

Application Deadline: January 15

Application link: https://www.barry.edu/en/stamps-scholars-program/

6 Stetson University

Location: DeLand, Florida
Setting: Suburban (185 Acres)
Undergraduate Enrollment: 3,125
Type: Private

J. Ollie Edmunds Distinguished Scholarship: This scholarship pays for all undergraduate expenses.

Requirements: A minimum SAT score of 1350 (critical reading and math) or an ACT composite score of 30 | A minimum GPA of 3.5

Application Deadline: January 8

Application link: https://www.stetson.edu/administration/financial-aid/scholarships/

FLORIDA

Rollins College

Location: Winter Park, Florida
Setting: Suburban (80 Acres)
Undergraduate Enrollment: 2,127
Type: Private

Alfond Scholars program: Full tuition, fees, room and board.

Requirements: 1450 or higher (Evidenced Based Reading and Math) or ACT's of 32 or higher.

Application Deadline: November 1

Application link: https://www.rollins.edu/financial-aid/as-cps-financial-aid/scholarships/

Webber International University

Location: Babson Park, Florida
Setting: Rural (110 Acres)
Undergraduate Enrollment: 748
Type: Private

Bright Futures Academic Scholarship: 100% average state university tuition – approx. $211 per credit hour + $300 Book stipend.

Requirements: 1330 SAT/ 29 ACT | 3.50 High school GPA.

Application Deadline: August 1

Application link: https://www.webber.edu/

University of South Florida

Location: Tampa, Florida
Setting: Urban (1,646 Acres)
Undergraduate Enrollment: 38,579
Type: Public

USF Tradition of Excellence Awards: Award covers the full cost of attendance.

Requirements: Applicant must be recognised as a National Merit Scholar Finalist by the National Merit Scholarship Corporation.

P.S: Semi-finalists are awarded $20,000 ($5,000 per year) until they are officially classified as a National Merit Finalist and select USF as their first-choice school.

Application Deadline: March 1

Application link: https://www.usf.edu/admissions/freshmen/admission-information/cost-of-attendance/scholarships.aspx

FLORIDA

University of Miami

Location: Coral Gables, Florida
Setting: Suburban (239 Acres)
Undergraduate Enrollment: 11,334
Type: Private

Stamps Scholarship: Award covers the full cost of attendance (includes tuition and fees, on-campus housing, a meal plan, University health insurance, textbooks, a laptop allowance, and access to a $12,000 enrichment fund which may be used for other educational purposes)
Requirements: Top Applicants.

George W. Jenkins Scholarship: Award covers the full cost of attendance which includes tuition and fees, on-campus housing, a meal plan, University health insurance, and a laptop allowance. Students may also receive a stipend for books, transportation, and personal expenses.
Criteria: To be considered for this scholarship, students must be nominated by their guidance counselor.

Application Deadline: November 1
Application links:
https://admissions.miami.edu/undergraduate/financial-aid/scholarships/freshman/index.html#

Florida A&M University

Location: Tallahassee, Florida
Setting: City (422 Acres)
Undergraduate Enrollment: 7,402
Type: Public

Presidential Special Scholarship: This scholarship cover fees associated with tuition, but minus the postal fee and the $35 orientation fee, it covers charges for room and board, but minus fines.

Requirements: U.S citizen or permanent resident | Have 1260 on the redesigned SAT or 27 on the ACT | Have a 3.5 FAMU recalculated GPA.

Medical Scholars Program: Full scholarship for both in-state and out-of-state students, Full tuition and fees, double occupancy room rate, and board plus other benefits.

Requirements: 3.5 GPA or higher | 1290 or better SAT score / 29 or better ACT score

Application Deadline: Contact fran.scott@famu.edu for more information.

Army ROTC, Air Force ROTC, Navy-Marine ROTC Scholarship programs all awards Full tuition, room and board, stipends for books, supplies and equipments, etc.

Application Deadline: September 4

Application link:
https://www.famu.edu/students/scholarships/index.php

FLORIDA

Florida International University

Location: Miami, Florida
Setting: Urban (344 Acres)
Undergraduate Enrollment: 48,664
Type: Public

FIU National Merit Finalist: Award covers Full tuition, Fees, plus a book stipend, 100% housing with meal plan, Laptop (with demonstration of financial need)

Requirements: Applicant must be recognised as a National Merit Scholar Finalist | U.S citizen, a U.S. lawful permanent resident or an international student with intention of receiving the F-1 visa to study in the United States.

Presidential Merit Scholarship: Awards Full tuition and fees, plus a book stipend.

Requirements: A minimum SAT score of 1370 or 30 ACT or Top 5% of a Florida High School Graduating Class | 4.0 GPA | U.S citizen, a U.S. lawful permanent resident or an international student with intention of receiving the F-1 visa to study in the United States.

FIU College Board Recognition Program Scholarship: Awards Full tuition, fees, book stipends, plus a $1,000 meal plan stipend per semester.

Requirements: Applicant must be awarded one of the recognition awards from the College Board | 4.0 weighted HS GPA | 1370 or SAT or 30 ACT.

Application Deadline: January 31

Application link: https://scholarships.fiu.edu/browse-scholarships/merit-scholarships/index.html

FLORIDA

13 University of Central Florida

Location: Orlando, Florida
Setting: Suburban (1,415 Acres)
Undergraduate Enrollment: 61,456
Type: Public

Benacquisto Scholarship: Awards full institutional cost of attendance for an in-state student minus the sum of Bright Futures and the National Merit award. Out-of-state students will receive an award equal to the in-state cost of attendance minus their National Merit award. These students are exempted from paying out-of-state tuition and fees.

Please refer to this site for eligibility requirements and more information: https://www.ucf.edu/financial-aid/types/scholarships/benacquisto/

Florida Academic Scholars: Award amount equal to 100% of tuition and applicable fees in fall, spring and summer.

Eligibility: Eligibility and application criteria are available from your high school guidance office, or the Florida Bright Futures Program website.

Application Deadline: August 31

Application link: https://www.ucf.edu/financial-aid/types/scholarships/florida-bright-futures/

FLORIDA

New College of Florida

Location: Sarasota, Florida
Setting: Suburban (110 Acres)
Undergraduate Enrollment: 646
Type: Public

Florida Freshmen

Florida Education Fund Brain Bowl Scholarship: Awards Full scholarship (tuition, room, and board)

Criteria: This scholarship is awarded to first-place team members of the statewide competition in mathematics and also first place team members in history and culture.

Out-of-State Freshmen

Benacquisto Scholar Award: Out-of-state students who qualify for the Benacquisto scholarship will receive an award equal to the in-state on-campus cost of attendance for New College, minus their National Merit award. Such students are exempt from paying the out-of-state fees. This scholarship covers the full cost of attendance.

Eligibility: Applicant must be recognised as a National Merit Finalist.

Application Deadline: April 1
Application link: https://www.ncf.edu/admissions/financial-aid/scholarships/

Florida Institute of Technology

Location: Melbourne, Florida
Setting: Suburban (174 Acres)
Undergraduate Enrollment: 3,475
Type: Private

Farmers Scholars Programs *(Available only to Florida Residents)*

Farmer Scholarship: Full tuition, room and board, and fees.

Requirements: Top applicants.

Application Deadline: February 1
Application link: https://www.fit.edu/admissions/applying/first-year/

GEORGIA

1. Emory University

Location: Atlanta, Georgia
Setting: City (631 Acres)
Undergraduate Enrollment: 7,010
Type: Private

Robert W. Woodruff Scholarship: Full tuition, room and board, lots more . . .

George W. Jenkins Scholarship: Full tuition, fees, on-campus room and board, and a stipend each semester, lots more . . .

Requirements: Top applicants

Application Deadline: November 15

Application links: https://studentaid.emory.edu/undergraduate/types/emory-college/grants-scholarships/index.html

Marvin B. Perry Presidential Scholarship: Full tuition, room and board.

Goizueta Foundation Scholarship: Full tuition, room and board.

Requirements: Top scholars.

Application Deadline: January 15

Application link: https://www.agnesscott.edu/admission/undergraduate-admission/scholarships-financial-aid/index.html

2. University of Georgia

Location: Athens, Georgia
Setting: City (767 Acres)
Undergraduate Enrollment: 29,765
Type: Public

While there are no available full ride scholarships at the University of Georgia, there are many other scholarships that could be highly beneficial to incoming freshmen.

Please refer to this site for more details: https://www.admissions.uga.edu/afford/scholarships/

3. Agnes Scott College

Location: Decatur, Georgia
Setting: Urban (100 Acres)
Undergraduate Enrollment: 1,014
Type: Private

GEORGIA

Point University

Location: West Point, Georgia
Setting: Suburban (54 Acres)
Undergraduate Enrollment: 2,340
Type: Private

Founders Scholarship: Awards Full tuition, fees, room and board.

P.S: Scholarship covers 15 – meal plan. Student will be required to pay difference if 19 – meal plan is selected.

Requirements: A minimum GPA of 3.5 | A combined SAT score of 1310 (Evidence-Based Reading and Writing, and Math) and an ACT score of 27 | Applicant should provide a written essay about why a Point University education is important and why he or she desires to attend the University.

P.S: Scholarships are awarded on a rolling basis, and decisions will be made the semester before your start date.

Application Deadline: Check site for more details.

Application link: https://point.edu/admissions/tuition-aid/financial-aid/scholarships/

LaGrange College

Location: LaGrange, Georgia
Setting: Rural (120 Acres)
Undergraduate Enrollment: 750
Type: Private

The Presidential Learning and Living Scholarship: Award covers Full tuition, fees, room and board.

Requirements: Top students

Application Deadline: January 1

Application link: https://www.lagrange.edu/admission-and-aid/financial-aid/types-of-aid/Scholarships.html

Mercer University

Location: Macon, Georgia
Setting: City (150 Acres)
Undergraduate Enrollment: 4,911
Type: Private

Stamps Scholars Program: Award covers Full tuition, fees, room and board, Apple iPad and up to $16,000 Enrichment stipend (to support Study Abroad, Undergraduate Research, Unpaid Internships, Conference Fees and Travel, etc.)

Requirements: Top applicants | Applicant must be a U.S. citizen or a permanent resident.

Application Deadline: November 15

Application link: https://www.stampsscholars.org/2012/11/01/mercer-university-macon-ga/

GEORGIA

Georgia Institute of Technology

Location: Atlanta, Georgia
Setting: Urban (400 Acres)
Undergraduate Enrollment: 16,561
Type: Public

Stamps President's Scholars Program: Full tuition, mandatory fees, housing, meal plan, books, and academics supplies, personal expenses, stipend for laptop, lots more...

Requirements: Semifinalist average SAT is 1450 - 1560 and ACT 33-35 | UK & US Citizens only.

Godbold Family Foundation: Godbold Scholars receive 100% of their financial need. The need is met with Institute gift aid that is matched with a Godbold Scholarship in combination with a $2,500 work study opportunity.

Requirements: Applicant must be an entering freshman from specific counties in South Carolina, Florida, North Carolina, and Tennessee | A minimum SAT score of 1500 (combination of math and verbal scores only) | Demonstrate financial need.

Gold Scholars Program: Awards Full tuition and fees *(to Georgia residents)*, a tuition waiver for *Out-of-State students*, Priority housing during your first year, plus a lot of other benefits.

P.S: *The package assumes the scholar has received the Zell Miller Scholarship independently from the state of Georgia.*

Criteria: This scholarship is offered annually to the top two percent of first-year students. Recipients are selected based upon holistic excellence and potential within the program's four pillars: Scholarship, Leadership, Progress, and Service.

Application Deadline: October 15

Application links: https://finaid.gatech.edu/undergraduate-types-aid/scholarships/institutional-scholarships#

GEORGIA

Wesleyan College

Location: Macon, Georgia
Setting: City (316 Acres)
Undergraduate Enrollment: 2,852
Type: Private

Peyton Anderson Scholarship: Full tuition plus room and board.

Eligibility: This is an annual scholarship for students from the Middle Georgia area who are committed to teaching in the middle Georgia area after graduation.

Requirements: Commitment to teach in Middle Georgia for five years | A minimum High school GPA of 3.6

Lovick P. and Elizabeth T. Corn Scholarship: Full tuition plus room and board.

Eligibility: This is an annual scholarship for students who demonstrate leadership in service to their schools, churches, or communities, and exemplify the qualities of leadership, character, and personal achievement.

Requirements: Applicant must be a graduate from any high school in Columbus, GA, or the greater Chattahoochee area | A minimum GPA of 3.20 (3.00 for Girls Inc.)

Application Deadline: February 15

Application links:
https://www.wesleyancollege.edu/admission/invitation-scholarships.cfm

Spelman College

Location: Atlanta, Georgia
Setting: Urban (39 Acres)
Undergraduate Enrollment: 2,207
Type: Private

Dovey Johnson Roundtree Scholarship: Full tuition, fees and on-campus room and board for four years.

Presidential Scholarship: Full tuition, fees and on-campus room and board for four years.

Requirements: A minimum SAT score of 1330 or 31 ACT | A minimum High school GPA of 3.8 (weighted)

Application Deadline: February 1

Application links:
https://www.spelman.edu/admissions/financial-aid/scholarships

Morehouse College

Location: Atlanta, Georgia
Setting: Urban (66 Acres)
Undergraduate Enrollment: 2,152
Type: Private

Morgan Stanley Student Success Scholarship: Award varies and scholars will receive funding for the **full cost of attendance** that is not already covered by other scholarships and financial aid.

Eligibility: Applicant's must be Incoming freshmen and Demonstrate financial need | 3.5 GPA | 1200+ SAT / 25+ ACT | Quality of submitted essay.

Dr. Michael L. Lomax Student Success Scholarship: Award will cover the **full cost of enrollment** and vary based on financial need.

Requirements: ACT 28+ / SAT 1000+ | A minimum cumulative high school GPA of 3.0 | Demonstrate low Expected Family Contribution (EFC) as illustrated on the Free Application for Federal Student Aid (FAFSA) and confirmed by the College's Office of Financial Aid.

SMASH Alumni Scholarship: Award covers the entire cost of enrollment (tuition, room and board expenses) after all Federal and State grants as well as private scholarships have been applied.

Eligibility: SMASH Alumnus | STEM Major | 2.5 GPA | Demonstrated Need (FAFSA required)

Application Deadline: April 14 / May 14

Application link:

https://www.morehouse.edu/admissions/financial-aid-and-scholarships/scholarships/

HAWAII

1. University of Hawaii

Location: Honolulu, Hawaii
Setting: Urban (320 Acres)
Undergraduate Enrollment: 13,203
Type: Public

The Regents and Presidential Scholarships covers the cost of tuition, and includes a $4000 stipend per year.

Eligibility: Regents Scholarships are awarded to outstanding freshmen who has a minimum SAT total score of at least 1340 or ACT combined score of at least 29 | A minimum High school GPA of 3.5

Application Deadline: January 15

Application link: https://www.hawaii.edu/offices/student-affairs/regents-and-presidential-scholars-program/

IDAHO

University of Idaho

Location: Moscow, Idaho
Setting: Rural (810 Acres)
Undergraduate Enrollment: 8,366
Type: Public

National Merit Scholarship: This award covers basic registration fees/tuition and the university defined cost for room and board as long as you live in a U of I residence hall.

Requirements: Achieve Finalist standing with the National Merit Scholarship Corporation.

Application Deadline: May 31

Application link: https://www.uidaho.edu/financial-aid/scholarships/undergraduate/hs-resident

ROTC Military Scholarships:

United States Army ROTC: This program offers 3.5 year, 3 year, 2.5 year and 2 year on campus scholarships that will pay for in/out state tuition and fees, pay $510 for books annually, and give at least $250 per month as a stipend while in school.

Call: University of Idaho Army ROTC for application at 208-885-6528

United States Air Force ROTC: This program offers scholarships to students who have at least two years remaining towards their bachelor degree when the scholarship starts. Awards full tuition, books, fees, and a monthly stipend during the academic year.

Call: University of Idaho Unit Admissions Officer, AFROTC Detachment 905, at 208-885-6129 or 800-622-5088.

United States Navy/Marine ROTC: This program offers scholarships to students selected through national competition. It covers college tuition, lab fees, books, uniforms, and includes a monthly stipend.

Call: University of Idaho, Commanding Officer, Naval Science Department at 208-885-6333.

Please refer to this site for more details: https://www.uidaho.edu/financial-aid/scholarships/undergraduate/hs-non-resident

ILLINOIS

1. University of Illinois

Location: Urbana-Champaign, Illinois
Setting: City (1,783 Acres)
Undergraduate Enrollment: 33,683
Type: Public

Stamps Scholarship: Awards up to the full cost of attendance.

James Hunter Anthony & Gerald E. Blackshear Endowment: Awards up to full tuition and fees for an academic year.

Requirements: Illinois Resident who have graduated from an Illinois high school | Top applicants.

Application Deadline: December 1

Application link: https://www.admissions.illinois.edu/invest/scholarships-all

2. University of Chicago

Location: Chicago, Illinois
Setting: Urban (217 Acres)
Undergraduate Enrollment: 6,989
Type: Private

University Merit Scholarships: The University Scholarship goes towards the full cost of attendance.

Uchicago Evans Scholarship: Awards full housing and tuition.

Requirements: Top scholars.

Application Deadline: December 1

Application link: https://collegeadmissions.uchicago.edu/financial-support/scholarships/merit-scholarships

3. Southern Illinois University Edwardsville

Location: Edwardsville, Illinois
Setting: Suburban (2,660 Acres)
Undergraduate Enrollment: 9,942
Type: Public

Meridian Scholarship: Full tuition, fees, room and board. This scholarship is available to both U.S citizens and International students.

Eligibility: Cumulative 3.5 high school GPA (4.0 scale) | A minimum SAT ERW + M of 1260 or ACT 27.

Application Deadline: November 15

Application link: https://www.siue.edu/financial-aid/types-of-aid/scholarships.shtml

ILLINOIS

4 Western Illinois University

Location: Macomb, Illinois
Setting: Rural (1,050 Acres)
Undergraduate Enrollment: 5,854
Type: Public

Presidential Scholarship: Full tuition, fees, a double residence hall room and meal plan.

Requirements: 3.6+ GPA | 1300+ SAT or 28+ ACT.

Application Deadline: December 1

Application link: http://www.wiu.edu/student_success/scholarship/

5 Southern Illinois University Carbondale

Location: Carbondale, Illinois
Setting: Rural (1,136 Acres)
Undergraduate Enrollment: 8,466
Type: Public

Chancellor's Scholarship: Covers in-state tuition, mandatory fees, room and board.

Requirements: 3.8+ GPA | Top applicants

Application Deadline: December 1

Application link: https://scholarships.siu.edu/types/freshmen-students.php

ILLINOIS

Illinois Institute of Technology

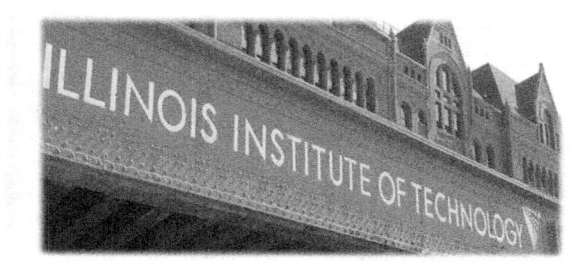

Location: Chicago, Illinois
Setting: Urban (120 Acres)
Undergraduate Enrollment: 3,123
Type: Private

Duchossois Leadership Scholars Program:

Full tuition, room and board

Eligibility: ACT/SAT scores in the top 10% nationally | A minimum 3.5 high school GPA.

Application Deadline: November 15

Application link:
https://www.iit.edu/admissions-aid/tuition-and-aid/scholarships

Trinity International University

Location: Deerfield, Illinois
Setting: Suburban (111 Acres)
Undergraduate Enrollment: 722
Type: Private

There are scholarships available for undergraduate studies at the Trinity International University.

Check site for more details.

Application link:
https://www.tiu.edu/divinity/scholarships-aid/

ILLINOIS

8 University of Illinois at Chicago

Location: Chicago, Illinois
Setting: Urban (240 Acres)
Undergraduate Enrollment: 21,921
Type: Public

President's Award Program (Honors Scholars Program): Awards Full tuition and housing, a week-long Summer College orientation Program, and a new laptop computer *(Illinois Resident's)*

Eligibility: Top applicants | Applicants must be Incoming freshmen and Demonstrate financial need | From an Illinois county with low representation in the University system.

Application Deadline: December 1
Application link: https://aes.uic.edu/programs/presidents-award-program.html

Dreamer Scholarship: Award covers Full tuition, on campus room and board, and mandatory student fees.

Eligibility: Applicants must exhibit excellence.

Application link: https://www.luc.edu/finaid/scholarships/undergraduate/

9 Loyola University Chicago

Location: Chicago, Illinois
Setting: City (105 Acres)
Undergraduate Enrollment: 11,612
Type: Private

ROTC Scholarships

Air Force ROTC Scholarship: Full tuition and Mandatory fees.

Army ROTC Scholarship: Full tuition and fees, $1,200 per year for books, plus a stipend ranging from $350 - $500 per school month. Additionally, Army ROTC Scholarship students receive $3,500 a semester toward on-campus housing from Loyola University.

Navy ROTC Scholarship: Full tuition and fees.

P.S: Students who receive full ROTC scholarships are also awarded a $3500 per semester ROTC On-Campus Housing Grant from Loyola University.

Please refer to this site for more details:

https://www.luc.edu/finaid/military/rotc-scholarships/

Application Deadline: December 1

INDIANA

1. Purdue University

Location: West Lafayette, Indiana
Setting: City (2,468 Acres)
Undergraduate Enrollment: 34,920
Type: Private

Beering Scholarship: Awards full ride scholarship to Top applicants.

Eligibility: Determined by the dean of enrollment services based on your admissions application.

Please refer to this site for more details:

https://engineering.purdue.edu/Engr/AboutUs/News/Announcements/10-incoming-engineering-students-receive-fullride-scholarships

2. University of Southern Indiana

Location: Evansville, Indiana
Setting: Suburban (330 Acres)
Undergraduate Enrollment: 6,739
Type: Public

Presidential Scholarship: Full tuition, room and board and book stipends.

Requirements: Indiana Residents | A minimum SAT score of 1200 / ACT score of 27 | Ranked first or second in their senior class.

Global Ambassador Scholarship: Full tuition, on-campus room and board.

Requirements: This scholarship is awarded to international students | A minimum of 3.5 High school GPA.

Application Deadline: December 4

Application link: https://www.usi.edu/financial-aid/aid/scholarships/freshmen-scholarships/

INDIANA

Ball State University

Location: Muncie, Indiana
Setting: Suburban (1,180 Acres)
Undergraduate Enrollment: 15,780
Type: Public

1) **Whitinger Scholarship**: Full tuition, mandatory fees, on-campus room and board.

2) **Presidential Scholarship**: Full tuition, fees, room and board.

3) **Ball State Scholars Award**: Full tuition, fees, room and board.

4) **Distinction Scholarship**: Full tuition, fees, room and board.

5) **Harold Ellison Scholarship**: Full tuition, room and board.

P.S: This scholarship is available only to first-time freshmen who have graduated from schools in Delaware County, Indiana.

Applicants must be nominated by their high school guidance counselor and only if they have already been awarded the Ball State Presidential Scholarship.

The deadline to apply is **February 1** of each year.

ROTC Scholarships are also available!

Requirements: Scholars must demonstrate a high degree of excellence.

Application Deadline: November 15

Application links: https://www.bsu.edu/admissions/financial-aid-and-scholarships/types/scholarships#accordion_ballstatescholarsaward

INDIANA

4 University of Indiana

Location: Bloomington, Indiana
Setting: City (1,944 Acres)
Undergraduate Enrollment: 32,986
Type: Public

Wells Scholars Program: Guarantees the full cost of attendance for a period of eight semesters of undergraduate study.

Award covers full tuition, mandatory and course-related fees, as well as living stipends during the fall and spring sufficient to cover the cost of a standard double dorm room contract and a standard meal plan in the residence halls.

P.S: Students receive the same stipend whether they choose to live on or off campus.

Requirements: Top applicants.

21st Century Scholarship Convenant: Available to scholars who demonstrate unmet financial need. Covers the cost of tuition and mandatory fees. Provides additional funding to assist with budgeted room and board, books, and supplies.

Requirements: Check site for more details.

Application Deadline: November 1

Application link: https://scholarships.indiana.edu/future-scholars/index.html

5 University of Notre Dame

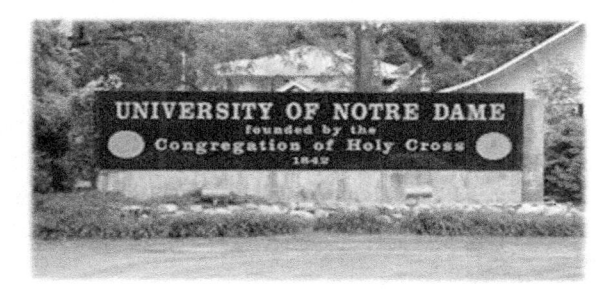

Location: Notre Dame, Indiana
Setting: Suburban (1,265 Acres)
Undergraduate Enrollment: 8,874
Type: Private

Glenna R. Joyce Scholarship: Full cost of attendance for four years.

Requirements: Top applicants | Must be residents of some specified states.

Western Golf Association Evans Foundation Scholarship: Awards Full tuition, mandatory fees and housing.

Please refer to this site for more details: https://scholars.nd.edu/awards/list-of-awards/western-golf-association-evans-foundation-scholarship/

Requirements: Top applicants

Application Deadline: November 1

Application link: https://scholars.nd.edu/awards/list-of-awards/

INDIANA

Wabash College

Location: Crawfordsville, Indiana
Setting: City (94 Acres)
Undergraduate Enrollment: 868
Type: Private

Wabash College Lilly Award: Full tuition, standard fees, on-campus room and board.

Requirements: A minimum GPA of 3.5 (4.0 scale) | An SAT score of at least 1240 or an ACT composite of 26 | Rank within the top 10 percent of your senior class.

Army ROTC Scholarship Program: Awards Full tuition, on-campus room and board as well as all costs associated with ROTC courses.

Scholarship Cadets are also given a book allowance of $600 per semester along with a $420 per month, tax free stipend allowance during each school year.

Requirements: Applicant must be a U.S citizen | A minimum cumulative high school GPA of 2.50 | Score minimum of 1000 on the SAT or 19 on the ACT | Meet the minimum physical standards of the Army physical fitness test.

Trustee International Scholarships: Awards Full tuition, fees, and on-campus room and board (*to international students*).

Please refer to this site for more details: https://www.wabash.edu/admissions/international

Requirements: Top scholars who demons

P.S: All international students with a complete admissions application on record by February 15 will be reviewed for the Trustee Scholarship Awards.

Application Deadline: January 6

Application link: https://www.wabash.edu/admissions/finances/sources

INDIANA

Valparaiso University

Location: Valparaiso, Indiana
Setting: City (350 Acres)
Undergraduate Enrollment: 2,723
Type: Private

Lilly Community Foundation Scholarship: Awards full tuition, fees, standard on-campus room and board plus a $900 per year stipend for required books and equipment.

Eligibility: **Indiana residents attending an Indiana high school.**

Requirements: Top students in application pool.

Army ROTC Scholarship Program: Awards Full tuition, fees, standard on-campus room and board, a book stipend and a monthly stipend.

P.S: Applicant must be a U.S citizen | Must apply to ROTC by December 1

Requirements: Top scholars.

Air Force ROTC Scholarship Program: Awards Full tuition, fees, standard on-campus room and board, a book stipend and a monthly stipend.

Requirements: Top applicants.

Application Deadline: March 1

Application link: https://www.valpo.edu/student-financial-services/planning/scholarships/other/

IOWA

1. Grand View University

Location: Des Moines, Iowa
Setting: Urban (25 Acres)
Undergraduate Enrollment: 1,757
Type: Private

Immigrant Iowan Scholarship: Award covers full tuition, room charges if the recipient lives on campus, plus some specified fees.

Eligibility: Applicant must be born of an immigrant parent or an immigrant himself or herself | Graduating from an Iowa high school | High school GPA of 3.0 or higher | Not in the U.S. on a student visa.

Presidential Scholarship aspirant's may compete for full tuition and additional $5,000 awards.

Application Deadline: March 1

Application link: https://www.grandview.edu/admissions/financial-aid/scholarships-grants#

2. Grinnell College

Location: Grinnell, Iowa
Setting: Rural (120 Acres)
Undergraduate Enrollment: 1,493
Type: Private

Laurel Scholarship and Mentorship Program: This is a Chicago-based, small mentorship program that offers pre-arrival programming, a full-tuition scholarship, and additional need-based financial aid to assist with the cost of room and board.

Eligibility: Applicant's Home address must be in the city of Chicago or Cook County, IL | Black or Afro-descendant | U.S. citizen or permanent resident.

Application Deadline: December 1

Application link: https://www.grinnell.edu/admission/financial-aid/affording-grinnell/scholarships

KANSAS

1. University of Saint Mary

Location: Leavenworth, Kansas
Setting: Rural (200 Acres)
Undergraduate Enrollment: 810
Type: Private

Jubilee Scholarship: Awards full tuition, room and board.

Requirements: A minimum ACT score of 26 or SAT equivalent | Have a 3.7 cumulative high school GPA (unweighted on a 4.0 scale) | Be ranked in the top 10 percent of your graduating high school class.

Please refer to this site for more details: https://www.stmary.edu/jubilee

---

The Sister Joanna Bruner Nursing Scholarship: Assists with educational expenses such as tuition, fees, room, board, and books.

Eligibility: A minimum ACT composite score of 21 or SAT equivalent | Applicant must be accepted to USM's Bachelor of Science-Nursing Program | Must live on campus | Must demonstrate financial need by completing the FASA.

Application Deadline: December 1
Application link: https://www.stmary.edu/scholarships

KENTUCKY

1. Bellarmine University

Location: Louisville, Kentucky
Setting: Urban (145 Acres)
Undergraduate Enrollment: 2,484
Type: Private

Bellarmine Scholar Award: Full ride scholarship plus study abroad stipend and enrollment into Bellarmine's Honors Program.

Requirements: An essay with the topic "Describe an incident or situation in your life which piqued your intellectual curiosity" | A minimum SAT score of 1390/ACT 30 & 3.5 GPA.

Application Deadline: February 1

Application link: https://www.bellarmine.edu/financial-aid/institutional/

2. Campbellsville University

Location: Campbellsville, Kentucky
Setting: Rural (95 Acres)
Undergraduate Enrollment: 5,794
Type: Private

Presidential Excellence: Full tuition, room and board.

Eligibility: Open to students who have 33-36 on ACT/ 2170-2400 SAT & 3.5 GPA.

Application Deadline: November 1

Application link: https://www.campbellsville.edu/admission-and-aid/scholarships-and-grants/

KENTUCKY

Center College

Location: Danville, Kentucky
Setting: City (178 Acres)
Undergraduate Enrollment: 1,333
Type: Private

Grissom Scholars: Award covers the full cost of attendance, plus additional aid to cover any remaining financial need. $5,000 enrichment funds.

Eligibility: All first-generation college students who apply for admission by January 15 will be considered automatically for the Grissom Scholars Program.

Please refer to this site for more details: centre.edu/grissom-scholars/

Brown Fellows: Covers full cost of attendance, including tuition, room and board, $10,000 in enrichment funds.

Requirements: 3.95 GPA | Graduating at or very near the top of their high school class.

N.B: Test scores are not required.

Application Deadline: February 1

Application link: https://www.centre.edu/scholarships/#

Kentucky Wesleyan College

Location: Owensboro, Kentucky
Setting: City (67 Acres)
Undergraduate Enrollment: 881
Type: Private

Kentucky Wesleyan Rogers' Fellows Scholarship: Full tuition, fees, room and board.

Eligibility: Applicant must be a graduate of the Clark Country School District in Las Vegas, Nevada.

Requirements: A minimum 2.5 cumulative high school GPA.

Application Deadline: March 1

Application link: https://kwc.edu/admissions/financial-aid/scholarships/

KENTUCKY

5. University of Kentucky

Location: Lexington, Kentucky
Setting: City (918 Acres)
Undergraduate Enrollment: 22,227
Type: Public

Otis A. Singletary: Full tuition + Housing Stipend. This scholarship is available to both in-state and out-of-state Residents.

Requirements: 33 ACT/1450 SAT | 3.8 GPA

Application Deadline: December 1

Application link: https://www.uky.edu/financialaid/scholarship-incoming-freshmen

6. University of Louisville

Location: Louisville, Kentucky
Setting: Urban (287 Acres)
Undergraduate Enrollment: 15,927
Type: Public

National Merit Finalist: Full in-state tuition, $8,000 educational allowance.

Martin Luther King Scholars Program: Full tuition, $8,000 educational allowance.

Requirements: 3.5 GPA | 26 ACT or 1230 SAT | Black/African-American and Hispanic/Latino students.

Mentored Scholarships for out-of-state students:

Brown Fellows Program: Full tuition, plus additional education allowance.

Please refer to this site for more details: https://louisville.edu/admissions/cost-aid/scholarships/out-of-state-scholarships

Requirements: 29 ACT or 1330 SAT | 3.5 GPA

Application Deadline: December 15

Application link: https://louisville.edu/admissions/cost-aid/scholarships/ky-so-in-scholarships

KENTUCKY

Kentucky State University

Location: Frankfort, Kentucky
Setting: City (916 Acres)
Undergraduate Enrollment: 2,148
Type: Public

Commonwealth Scholarship: Full tuition, course fees, room and board, provides a stipend for books and supplies per semester.

Requirements: Residents of Kentucky | A minimum GPA of 3.2 (4.0 Scale) | Rank in 10% of graduating class.

Presidential Scholarship: Full tuition, course fees, room and board, provides a stipend for books and supplies per semester.

Requirements: A minimum SAT score of 1170/ACT 26 | 3.5 GPA or higher.

Check out this Scholarship Handbook for a comprehensive list of available scholarships: https://www.kysu.edu/wp-content/uploads/2013/10/Scholarship-16.pdf

John Henry Jackson Scholarship : Full tuition and mandatory fees, standard housing, meals and books.

Requirements: A minimum 3.5 cumulative high school GPA | A minimum 25 ACT or SAT equivalent.

Application Deadline: February 15

Application link: https://www.kysu.edu/finance-and-administration/financial-aid/scholarships.php

KENTUCKY

8 Lindsey Wilson College

Location: Columbia, Kentucky
Setting: Rural (200 Acres)
Undergraduate Enrollment: 1,974
Type: Private

Begley Scholarship: Awards full tuition, fees, room & board. If a student chooses to commute, the scholarship will cover tuition and fees only.

Requirements: A minimum high school GPA of 3.0 | A minimum ACT composite score of 24.

P.S: A typewritten essay (one to two pages in length) on a topic chosen by the scholarship committee is required.

Application Deadline: Check site for more details.

Application link:
https://academiccatalog.umd.edu/undergraduate/fees-expenses-financial-aid/merit-based-financial-assistance/

9 Murray State University

Location: Murray, Kentucky
Setting: Rural (253 Acres)
Undergraduate Enrollment: 7,939
Type: Public

National Merit Finalist Scholarship: Awards Full tuition, On-campus housing (double occupancy) and Meal plan.

Requirements: Awarded to National Merit Finalists.

Presidential Fellowship: Awards Full tuition, On-campus housing (double occupancy) and Meal plan.

Requirements: A minimum of 28 ACT composite score (or minimum of 1300 SAT Verbal and Math Combined Score) | A 3.7 cumulative high school GPA on a 4.0 scale.

Marvin D. Mills Scholarship: Awards Full tuition (equal to Kentucky cost of tuition), On-campus housing (double occupancy) and a Meal plan.

Requirements: A minimum of 24 ACT composite score or SAT equivalent | A 3.2 cumulative high school GPA on a 4.0 scale.

Application Deadline: December 1

Application link:
https://www.murraystate.edu/admissions/scholarships/newfreshmen.aspx

LOUISIANA

1. Xavier University

Location: New Orleans, Louisiana
Setting: Urban (66 Acres)
Undergraduate Enrollment: 2,517
Type: Private

Board of Trustees Scholarship: Awards full tuition, fees, and room & board to top applicants.

Presidential Scholarship: Full tuition and fees.

Saint Katharine Drexel Scholarship: Awards full tuition and fees to students who attend a Catholic high school within the United States and are the Valedictorian or Salutatorian of their high school graduating class.

Norman C. Francis Scholarship: Awards full tuition and fees to students who attend a public high school within Orleans or Jefferson Parishes and are the Valedictorian or Salutatorian of their high school graduating class.

P.S: There are some Specific Requirements for some of the listed scholarships.

Requirements: A minimum 3.3 GPA | 22 ACT/1140 SAT.

Application Deadline: January 31

Application link: https://www.xula.edu/academic-scholarships/

2. Louisiana Sate University

Location: Baton Rouge, Louisiana
Setting: Urban (2,000 Acres)
Undergraduate Enrollment: 27,825
Type: Public

Stamps Scholarship: Full tuition, fees, room & board, books, supplies, etc.

A potential $14,000 for enrichment experiences | The opportunity to earn up to an additional $1,550 per year by participating in the President's Future Leaders in Research program. | A one-time use $1,100 laptop stipend.

The President's Alumni Scholars Award: Full tuition, fees, room & board, books, supplies, etc.

$2,000 study abroad stipend | The opportunity to earn up to an additional $1,550 per year by participating in the President's Future Leaders in Research program.

Requirements: Top Applicants.

Application Deadline: December 15

Application link: https://www.lsu.edu/financialaid/types_of_scholarships/entering_freshman_scholarships/top-merit-based-scholarships.php

LOUISIANA

Tulane University of Louisiana

Location: New Orleans, Louisiana
Setting: Urban (110 Acres) Undergraduate
Enrollment: 7,700
Type: Private

Stamps Scholarship: Award covers the total cost of attendance and provides an enrichment fund to support endeavours such as study abroad, undergraduate research, academic or co-curricular conferences, and unpaid internships.

P.S: Select Stamps Finalists will be invited to interview in early spring.

John Hainkel Louisiana Scholars Award: Full tuition, room and board plus a stipend for books and other expenses.

Eligibility: Students who finish in the top 5% of their class while taking an honors or AP course load are eligible for this scholarship.

P.S: To be eligible, students must submit for early admission and submit the Dean's scholarship application and have a sealed scholarship recommendation from one of their educators.

Application Deadline: January 15
Application link: https://admission.tulane.edu/tuition-aid

LOUISIANA

4. Dillard University

Location: New Orleans, Louisiana
Setting: Urban (55 Acres)
Undergraduate Enrollment: 1,215
Type: Private

University Scholarship: Full tuition, room and board and mandatory fees.

Requirements: A minimum 3.8 cumulative high school GPA (4.0 scale) | A minimum 27 ACT composite score or 1220 SAT combined score.

Application Deadline: March 15

Application link: https://www.dillard.edu/financialaid/institutional-scholarships.php

5. Louisiana Tech University

Location: Ruston, Louisiana
Setting: Rural (2,277 Acres)
Undergraduate Enrollment: 10,289
Type: Public

National Merit Scholarship: Full tuition, fees, on-campus housing, and meals.

Awarded to are National Merit Finalists.

Requirements: A minimum 3.0 cumulative high school GPA (4.0 unweighted scale)

Application Deadline: Apply for admission according to National Merit deadlines.

Application link: https://www.latech.edu/admissions/freshman-scholarships/

MAINE

1. University of Southern Maine

Location: Portland, Maine
Setting: City (142 Acres)
Undergraduate Enrollment: 6,098
Type: Public

The Promise Scholarship: This Scholarship is designed to help students overcome financial and academic barriers. Awards will ensure any gaps are met to cover the full cost of tuition and fees.

Eligibility: Student must demonstrate a high financial need.

Preferences Include: Students referred from a Promise Partner Youth Development Organization and First-generation students.

Application Deadline: March 15

Application link: https://usm.maine.edu/scholarships/promise-scholarship

2. University of Maine

Location: Orono, Maine
Setting: Rural (660 Acres)
Undergraduate Enrollment: 9,465
Type: Public

Scholarship Programs for *Maine Residents*

UMaine National Merit Award: Awards Full tuition, fees, standard room and board.

Eligibility: Applicant should be a Semi-finalist with the National Merit Scholarship Corporation.

Scholarship Programs for *Out-of-State Residents*

Presidential Flagship: Award range from $20,000 to Full tuition and fees.

Requirements: Top applicants.

P.S: *Semi-finalists with the National Merit Scholarship Corporation are eligible for the highest awards in this category, **including: 100% Tuition and fees, up to 15 credits per semester, & standard room and board.***

Application Deadline: December 1

Application link: https://go.umaine.edu/apply/scholarships/

MARYLAND

1. Coppin State University

Location: Baltimore, Maryland
Setting: Urban (38 Acres)
Undergraduate Enrollment: 2,108
Type: Public

Presidential Scholarship: Awards Full tuition, room, board, fees, insurance fee, and up to $2,000/year for books.

Requirements: A weighted high school cumulative grade point average of 3.5 or above | A minimum 1200 SAT score or an ACT composite score of 25.

Fanny Jackson Coppin Scholarship: Awards Full tuition, room, board, and up to $1000/year for books.

Requirements: A weighted high school cumulative grade point average of 3.3 or above | A minimum 1140 SAT score or an ACT composite score of 23.

2. Washington College

Location: Chestertown, Maryland
Setting: Rural (112 Acres)
Undergraduate Enrollment: 1,089
Type: Private

Washington Scholars Program: Awards full tuition and fees, as well as room and board.

Please refer to this site for more details: https://www.washcoll.edu/admissions/washington-scholars.php

P.S: Applicant must demonstrate financial need.

Eligibility: Prospective Washington Scholars must be nominated by their high school counselors, community-based organization leaders, teachers, or their admissions counselors in order to be considered.

Application Deadline: January 15

Application link: https://www.washcoll.edu/admissions/admitted/available-scholarships.php

---

Army ROTC Scholarship: Awards full tuition, required educational fees, and provides a specified amount for books, supplies, and equipment. Each scholarship also includes a monthly stipend of $300 to $500 depending on your academic classification.

Requirements: A minimum 2.5 cumulative high school GPA | A minimum 920 SAT or composite 19 ACT score no later then November of the year you apply.

Check site for more details.

Application Deadline: October 1

Application link: https://www.coppin.edu/tuition-and-aid/scholarships-and-scholars-programs

MARYLAND

3. Loyola University Maryland

Location: Baltimore, Maryland
Setting: Urban (80 Acres)
Undergraduate Enrollment: 3,822
Type: Private

Army ROTC Scholarship: Awards Full tuition, fees, books and supplies. Recipients also receive a tax-free subsistence allowance each month that the recipient attends classes (up to 10 months each year)

Requirements: Top applicants.

Application Deadline: January 15

Application link: https://www.loyola.edu/department/financial-aid/undergraduate/programs/scholarships

4. McDaniel College

Location: Westminster, Maryland
Setting: Suburban (160 Acres)
Undergraduate Enrollment: 1,680
Type: Private

The Dorsey Scholars Program: Awards full tuition, room and board. In addition, Dorsey scholars also receive a stipend for books (up to $600 per semester), technology (up to $2000), and travel to McDaniel College Europe in Budapest (up to $2000).

Requirements: Student must exhibit excellence

Application Deadline: December 15

Application link: https://www.mcdaniel.edu/admissions-cost/cost-financial-aid/types-financial-aid/mcdaniel-scholarships

5. University of Maryland

Location: College park, Maryland
Setting: Suburban (1,335 Acres)
Undergraduate Enrollment: 30,875
Type: Private

Banneker/key Scholarship: Awards full tuition, mandatory fees, room & board, and book allowance each year for eight undergraduate consecutive semesters.

Requirements: Top applicants.

Application Deadline: November 1

Application link: https://academiccatalog.umd.edu/undergraduate/fees-expenses-financial-aid/merit-based-financial-assistance/

MASSACHUSETTS

1. Boston college

Location: Newton, Massachusetts
Setting: Suburban (376 Acres)
Undergraduate Enrollment: 9,445
Type: Private

Trustee Scholarship: Full tuition and fees.

Requirements: Top Students | Complete the Trustee scholarship essay.

The Gabelli Presidential Scholars program awards full tuition and fully funded scholarships. Please refer to this site for more details: https://www.bc.edu/bc-web/academics/sites/gabelli-presidential-scholars-program.html#

Application Deadline: December 1

Application link: https://www.bu.edu/admissions/tuition-aid/scholarships-financial-aid/first-year-merit/

2. Northeastern University

Location: Boston, Massachusetts
Setting: Urban (73 Acres)
Undergraduate Enrollment: 15,156
Type: Private

Torch Scholars Program: Full tuition, fees, room and board as well as significant personal and academic support.

Eligibility: Students must be nominated by an education professional, such as a guidance counselor.

Application Deadline: January 1

Application link: https://admissions.northeastern.edu/academics/honors-scholars-programs/

3. Simmons University

Location: Boston, Massachusetts
Setting: Urban (12 Acres)
Undergraduate Enrollment: 1,744
Type: Private

Kotzen Scholarship: Full tuition, room and board, plus an additional $3000 for academic pursuits such as study abroad, research support, and more.

Requirements: A minimum SAT score of 1300/ ACT 28 | 3.3 GPA or higher.

Application Deadline: December 1

Application link: https://www.simmons.edu/undergraduate/admission-and-financial-aid/tuition-financial-aid/types-financial-aid/scholarships/kotzen

MASSACHUSETTS

4 Clark University

Location: Worcester, Massachusetts
Setting: City (50 Acres)
Undergraduate Enrollment: 2,241
Type: Private

Presidential LEEP Scholarship: Full tuition, on-campus room and board for all four years, regardless of a family financial need.

Requirements: Top applicants | Applicant's must submit two additional scholarship essays.

Application Deadline: December 1

Application link: https://www.clarku.edu/offices/financial-aid/prospective-students/u-s-students/first-year-scholarships/

5 Framingham State University

Location: Framingham, Massachusetts
Setting: Suburban (77 Acres)
Undergraduate Enrollment: 3,520
Type: Public

The Mancuso English, Humanities, and social & Behavioral Sciences Scholarships: 100% of Day Division tuition, fees and room and board for Mancuso Scholars.

Eligibility: Applicant must graduate from a Massachusetts High School | Apply to the English major or specified FSU Humanities/Social & Behavioral Sciences major on the application for admissions | Have a minimum GPA of 3.5 at the time of application.

Application Deadline: November 15

Application link: https://www.framingham.edu/admissions-and-aid/financial-aid/types-of-aid/scholarships/index

6 University of Massachusetts - Lowell

Location: Lowell, Massachusetts
Setting: City (142 Acres)
Undergraduate Enrollment: 14,172
Type: Public

Tsongas Scholarship: Awards Full tuition, fees and standard room/board.

P.S: Applicants are selected by Lowell High School & the UMass Lowell committee.

Eligibility: Open to Massachusetts residents and Lowell High School graduates.

Application Deadline: November 5

Application link: https://www.uml.edu/thesolutioncenter/financial-aid/scholarships/freshmen.aspx

MICHIGAN

1. Northern Michigan University

Location: Marquette, Michigan
Setting: City (360 Acres)
Undergraduate Enrollment: 6,734
Type: Public

Presidential Scholars competition: Awards full ride scholarships to graduating high school seniors.

Requirements: To apply for the scholarship competition, students must be admitted and have an ACT composite score of 24 or higher or an SAT minimum score of 1160 and a minimum 3.5 GPA (4.0 scale)

Harden Scholarship: Full tuition, room and board, mandatory fees, and MacBook Pro fee (Art and Design majors)

Requirements: Top students in application pool

Presidential Scholarship: Full tuition, mandatory fees, and MacBook fee (Art and Design majors)

Requirements: Top Applicants

Application Deadline: October 15

Application link: https://nmu.edu/financialaid/nmugrants

2. Eastern Michigan University

Location: Ypsilanti, Michigan
Setting: City (460 Acres)
Undergraduate Enrollment: 13,572
Type: Public

Presidential Scholarship: Full tuition, room and board.

Requirements: A minimum 3.5 cumulative high school GPA | 1200+ SAT/ 25+ ACT (highest composite)

Application Deadline: December 1

Application link: https://www.emich.edu/admissions/undergraduate/first-year/scholarships.php

MICHIGAN

4. Central Michigan University

Location: Mount Pleasant, Michigan
Setting: Rural (480 Acres)
Undergraduate Enrollment: 13,048
Type: Public

Centralis Scholar Award: Full tuition, fees, on-campus room and board, books, and a $500 allowance toward the cost of books and supplies. Plus a $5,000 study away award.

Requirements: A minimum 3.7 high school GPA | 1260 SAT or 27 ACT.

Application Deadline: December 1

Application link: https://www.cmich.edu/offices-departments/office-scholarships-financial-aid/scholarships/scholarships-for-new-students

5. Lawrence Technological University

Location: Southfield, Michigan
Setting: Suburban (107 Acres)
Undergraduate Enrollment: 2,138
Type: Private

Donley Scholarship: Full tuition, room, board, books and fees for 4 years.

Requirements: High School GPA of 3.5 or higher | Major in the College of Engineering | Demonstrate high Financial need by means of the FAFSA.

Application Deadline: February 1

Application link: https://www.ltu.edu/financial_aid/scholarships.asp

6. Kalamazoo College

Location: Kalamazoo, Michigan
Setting: City (60 Acres)
Undergraduate Enrollment: 1,451
Type: Private

Heyl Scholarship: Provides support for students graduating from Kalamazoo Public Schools. This scholarship covers full tuition, room, fees, and provides a book allowance.

P.S: It does not cover board. It covers tuition and fees for study abroad programs.

Requirements: Top scholars in application pool.

Application Deadline: October 14

Application link: https://admission.kzoo.edu/cost-value/

MICHIGAN

7. Michigan State University

Location: East Lansing, Michigan
Setting: Suburban (5,192 Acres)
Undergraduate Enrollment: 38,491
Type: Public

Alumni Distinguished Scholarship: Full tuition, fees, room and board, and $1,000 annually.

Requirements: Scholars are expected to exhibit all-round excellence.

Application Deadline: November 1

Application link: https://admissions.msu.edu/cost-aid/scholarships/first-year

8. Michigan Technological University

Location: Houghton, Michigan
Setting: Rural (925 Acres)
Undergraduate Enrollment: 5,764
Type: Public

Leading Scholar Award:

Value for Michigan Resident's: Full tuition, room and board, and $1,000 to put towards fees and other expenses.

Value for Non-Michigan Resident's: Full tuition.

Requirements: Top applicants.

Application Deadline: October 15

Application link: https://www.mtu.edu/finaid/types/scholarships/

10. Davenport University

Location: Grand Rapids, Michigan
Setting: Suburban (77 Acres)
Undergraduate Enrollment: 4,999
Type: Private

Gerald R. Ford Memorial Scholarship: Awards Full tuition, books, fees, a study abroad experience, on-campus housing and meal plans.

Requirements: A minimum 3.75 cumulative high school GPA | A minimum 1430 SAT or 31 ACT.

Application Deadline: December 15

Application link: https://www.davenport.edu/financial-aid/scholarships

MICHIGAN

10 University of Michigan

Location: Ann Arbor, Michigan
Setting: City (3,207 Acres)
Undergraduate Enrollment: 31,329
Type: Public

Stamps Scholarship: Awarded to incoming U-M students, the College of LSA nominates a select number of incoming LSA students to receive this award.

Award amounts can go up to the full cost of attendance plus additional funding of up to $5,000 to support study abroad, community service, research, and internships.

Requirements: Top students in applicants pool.

Please refer to this site to Learn about the steps you need to take to be automatically considered for undergraduate scholarships at the University of Michigan: https://finaid.umich.edu/types-aid/scholarships/undergraduate

Application link: https://lsa.umich.edu/scholarships/prospective-students/merit-scholarships.html

11 Albion College

Location: Albion, Michigan
Setting: Suburban (574 Acres)
Undergraduate Enrollment: 1,475
Type: Private

Kalamazoo Promise: Students may have up to 100% of their financial need met to cover tuition, fees, housing and food costs.

Eligibility: Available to students who have the Kalamazoo Promise scholarship.

Application Deadline: February 15

Application link: https://www.albion.edu/offices/financial-aid/aid-scholarships/scholarships/

MICHIGAN

12. Wayne State University

Location: Detroit, Michigan
Setting: Urban (190 Acres)
Undergraduate Enrollment: 17,513
Type: Public

Wayne Med-Direct Scholars: Awards Full tuition, room and board, plus other benefits.

P.S: Awarded to students who wishes to pursue a career in Medicine.

Requirements: A minimum 3.5 cumulative high school GPA | A minimum 1310 SAT or 28 ACT score | Applicant must be a U.S. citizen or permanent resident.

Application Deadline: December 1
Application link:
https://provost.wayne.edu/wayne-med-direct

13. Lake Superior State University

Location: Sault Ste. Marie, Michigan
Setting: Rural (115 Acres)
Undergraduate Enrollment: 1,909
Type: Public

Laker Gold Scholarship Competition

Laker Premium: Full Ride (12-16 credits tuition + base rate room & board)

Requirements: A minimum 3.5 cumulative high school GPA | Top Applicants.

Application Deadline: December 15
Application link:
https://www.lssu.edu/financial-aid/types-of-aid/scholarships/

MINNESOTA

1. Concordia College

Location: Moorhead, Minnesota
Setting: Suburban (113 Acres)
Undergraduate Enrollment: 1,943
Type: Private

Community Access Scholarship: Awards Full tuition, comprehensive fees, room, and board.

Requirements: Top students

P.S: This scholarship is open to first-generation college-bound students from ethnically and socioeconomically diverse backgrounds who **live in Fargo-Moorhead** or the surrounding area and have a desire to achieve a four-year degree.

Application Deadline: February 28

Application link: https://www.concordiacollege.edu/tuition-aid/scholarships/concordia-scholarships/

2. University of Minnesota Twin Cities

Location: The Twin Cities of Minneapolis and Saint Paul, Minnesota
Setting: Urban (1,204 Acres)
Undergraduate Enrollment: 36,061
Type: Public

College of Science and Engineering

Clifford I. and Nancy C. Anderson Scholarship: Award covers the full cost of attendance.

Criteria for consideration is based on financial need.

Sezzle Scholarship: Award covers the full cost of attendance.

Criteria for consideration is based on financial need.

P.S: Preference for students interested in computer science, computer engineering, and data sciences | Preference for students from MN, North Dakota, South Dakota, and Wisconsin.

Application Deadline: November 1

Application link: https://admissions.tc.umn.edu/cost-aid/scholarships

MISSISSIPPI

1. Mississippi Valley State University

Location: Itta Bena, Mississippi
Setting: Rural (450 Acres)
Undergraduate Enrollment: 1,694
Type: Public

University Scholarship: This scholarship covers ½ tuition and fees and a book allowance of $200.

Requirements: 3.0 GPA or higher | ACT score of 20-21 or SAT equivalent.

Presidential Scholarship: Full tuition, room, board, fees and a book allowance of $500

Requirements: A minimum ACT score of 24 or SAT equivalent | 3.0 GPA

Vice President's Scholarship: Full tuition and fees and a book allowance of $300.

Requirements: A minimum ACT score of 22-23 or SAT equivalent | 3.0 GPA

Application Deadline: February 1

Application link:
https://www.mvsu.edu/prospective-students/scholarships

2. Mississippi State University

Location: Starkville, Mississippi
Setting: Rural (4,200 Acres)
Undergraduate Enrollment: 18,803
Type: Public

Presidential Scholarship Award: Full tuition, fees, room and board, research fellowships, and books for four years.

Non-resident students may also receive a scholarship to cover up to 100% of the out-of-state portion of tuition.

Requirements: A minimum 1330 SAT/ 30 ACT | 3.75 High school GPA or higher.

Application Deadline: December 1

Application link:
https://www.honors.msstate.edu/scholarships/

MISSISSIPPI

University of Mississippi

Location: Oxford, Mississippi
Setting: Rural (3,804 Acres)
Undergraduate Enrollment: 16,179
Type: Public

Stamps Scholarship: Awards up to the full cost of attendance after other awards. The package includes a $12,000 stipend for educational activities outside the classroom, including study abroad, research, and other enrichment pursuits.

Requirements: Entering freshmen with exceptional academic and leadership records.

Application Deadline: January 5

Academic Excellence Scholarship National Merit Semifinalist/Finalist Award: Awards full tuition, standard cost of a double occupancy room in a campus residence hall, covers full non-resident fee if applicable.

Eligibility: Entering freshmen with National Merit Semifinalist/Finalist status and a 3.0 or higher GPA.

Application Deadline: Follows National Merit announcement timeline.

Ole Miss Opportunity Program:

Eligible Mississippi resident students will receive financial aid support to cover the average cost of tuition, residence hall housing, and an allowance for meals.

Eligibility: Applicant must be a Mississippi resident and a U.S citizen | A minimum 3.0 high school GPA.

Application link: https://finaid.olemiss.edu/scholarships/

Jackson State University

Location: Jackson, Mississippi
Setting: Urban (220 Acres)
Undergraduate Enrollment: 4,668
Type: Public

Presidential Academic Scholarship: Award covers Full tuition, fees, room & board, and $750 per semester for books (campus only)

Requirements: ACT score of 28 or above or the SAT score of 1300 and above | 3.50 high school GPA.

Provost Academic Scholarship: Award covers Full tuition, room & board (campus charges only)

Requirements: ACT score of 25-27 or SAT score of 1200-1290 | 3.25 high school GPA.

Application Deadline: February 15

Application link: https://sites.jsums.edu/scholarships/

MISSISSIPPI

5. Rust College

Location: Holly Springs, Mississippi
Setting: Rural (126 Acres)
Undergraduate Enrollment: 738
Type: Private

Honor's Track Scholarship: Awards Holistic Full Scholarships

Requirements: A minimum 3.50 high school GPA.

Application Deadline: December 1

Application link: https://www.rustcollege.edu/prospective-students/financial-aid/scholarships/

6. University of Southern Mississippi

Location: Hattiesburg, Mississippi
Setting: Suburban (1,090 Acres)
Undergraduate Enrollment: 11,451
Type: Public

Presidential National Merit Finalist Scholarship: Award covers full tuition (and nonresident fees, if applicable), campus housing, a semester book stipend, and a meal plan for four years. Finalists will further receive a $4,000 study-abroad scholarship to participate in a Southern Miss study abroad program of their choice.

Eligibility: National Merit Finalist.

Presidential Scholarship: Award covers full tuition (and nonresident fees, if applicable), campus housing, a semester book stipend, and a meal plan for four years.

Requirements: A minimum 3.0 cumulative high school GPA | A minimum ACT composite score of 30 or a combined SAT score of 1330 excluding the written portion of the SAT.

Check site for more details.

Application Deadline: January 15

Application link: https://catalog.usm.edu/content.php?catoid=9&navoid=515

MISSOURI

1. Maryville University

Location: St. Louis, Missouri
Setting: Suburban (130 Acres)
Undergraduate Enrollment: 5,504
Type: Private

Presidential Scholarship: Full tuition, room and board.

Requirements: A minimum 3.75 cumulative high school GPA | 1290+ SAT / 27+ ACT

Dr. Donald M. Suggs Scholarship: Full tuition, room and board.

Eligibility: African American students from the St. Louis metropolitan area who have a minimum GPA of 3.25 | 1040+ SAT / 23+ ACT.

Application Deadline: December 1

Application link: https://www.maryville.edu/admissions/financial-aid/scholarships/

Presidential Honors Scholarship: Full tuition, room and board.

Requirements: Two letters of recommendation from high school teachers | GPA 3.8+ | ACT 32/ SAT 1450 Recommended – Not Required | 300-500 word personal statement as described within application.

2. Williams Wood University

Location: Fulton, Missouri
Setting: Rural (200 Acres)
Undergraduate Enrollment: 873
Type: Private

Amy Shelton McNutt: Full Tuition, room and board for 4 years.

Requirements: A minimum ACT score of 31 or SAT 1420 | 3.75 GPA.

Application Deadline: February 15

Application link: https://www.williamwoods.edu/admissions/undergraduate/scholarships/index.html

3. Park University

Location: Parkville, Missouri
Setting: Suburban (700 Acres)
Undergraduate Enrollment: 8,504
Type: Private

Application Deadline: November 1

Application link: https://www.park.edu/academics/honors-academy/scholarships/

MISSOURI

4. University of Missouri – Kansas City

Location: Kansas City, Missouri
Setting: Urban (150 Acres)
Undergraduate Enrollment: 11,036
Type: Public

Trustees Scholars Program: Awards Full tuition and fees, $500 towards books, on-campus room and board for a standard double room in Oak Street Residence Hall, and a $2,000 stipend toward living expenses in years three and four.

Requirements: A minimum 3.5 cumulative high school GPA in 17-class core curriculum | A minimum ACT composite score of 30 | Rank in the top 5% of your high school graduating class.

Eligibility: U.S. citizen or permanent residents.

Application Deadline: December 1

Application link:
https://finaid.umkc.edu/financial-aid/scholarships/

Sibley Scholarship: Awarded in a range and could cover up to full tuition, room and board.

Requirements: A minimum cumulative unweighted 3.50 high school GPA (on a 4.0 scale) | Submit a resume and a personal essay.

5. Truman State University

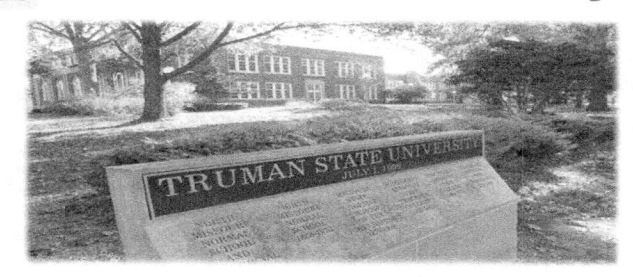

Location: Kirksville, Missouri
Setting: Rural (210 Acres)
Undergraduate Enrollment: 4,389
Type: Public

General John J. Pershing: Awards Full Tuition, on-campus room and meal plan annually, plus a one-time $4,000 study abroad stipend.

Requirements: Applicants should be in the top 3% of their HS class with ACT or SAT scores in the top 3% nationally.

Application Deadline: January 15

Application link:
https://www.truman.edu/admission-cost/cost-aid/scholarships/

6. Lindenwood University

Location: Saint Charles, Missouri
Setting: Suburban (285 Acres)
Undergraduate Enrollment: 4,822
Type: Private

Application Deadline: January 8

Application link:
https://www.lindenwood.edu/admissions/student-financial-services/scholarships-grants/

MISSOURI

7. Missouri State University

Location: Springfield, Missouri
Setting: City (225 Acres)
Undergraduate Enrollment: 19,801
Type: Public

Presidential Scholarship: Awards $15,000 per year ($7,000 for tuition and $8,000 for on-campus housing).

P.S: Non-Missouri residents will also receive a full waiver of nonresident fees for fall and spring semesters.

Requirements: A minimum 3.90 high school GPA at 6th semester | 31 ACT or 1390 SAT

Check site for more details.

Application Deadline: December 1

Application link: https://www.missouristate.edu/FinancialAid/scholarships/Freshman.htm

8. University of Missouri, Columbia

Location: Columbia, Missouri
Setting: City (1,262 Acres)
Undergraduate Enrollment: 23,396
Type: Public

Stamps Scholars Award: Awards full scholarship (up to estimated cost of attendance) plus a one-time award of $16,000 for academic development and leadership.

Requirements: 32-36 ACT or 1420-1600 SAT | 3.5 core HS GPA.

National Merit Finalist & Semifinalist Scholarship: Awards full tuition and fees, a $3,500 additional stipend plus a $10,964 one year on-campus housing and dining, a one time payment of $2,000 for research/study abroad and a $1,000 for tech enrichment.

Eligibility: Applicant must be deemed a National Merit Finalist or Semifinalist by the National Merit Scholarship Corporation (NMSC) | Awarded to *Missouri residents*.

Application Deadline: December 1

Application link: https://admissions.missouri.edu/scholarships/#auto_missouri

MONTANA

1 Montana State University

Location: Bozeman, Montana
Setting: City (1,780 Acres)
Undergraduate Enrollment: 14,240
Type: Public

Army ROTC Scholarship: Full tuition and mandatory fees or $10,000/year for room and board, a yearly book allowance ($1,200/year) and a tax free monthly stipend ($425/month)

Eligibility: Award is based on college performance (academics, physical fitness and standing in program)

Check site for more details.

Application link:
http://www.montana.edu/admissions/scholarships/additional.html

2 University of Providence

Location: Great Falls, Montana
Setting: City (44 Acres)
Undergraduate Enrollment: 790
Type: Private

Institutional Scholarships

The generous merit and athletic scholarships range from $11,000 – *Full Ride*.

Merit scholarship amounts for freshmen are determined by each student's high school academic performance.

Athletic scholarships are determined by the coach of each sports team and take the place of a merit scholarship on a financial aid offer.

Check site for more details.

Application link:
https://www.uprovidence.edu/financial-services/scholarships/

Nebraska Wesleyan University

Location: Lincoln, Nebraska
Setting: City (50 Acres)
Undergraduate Enrollment: 1,773
Type: Private

Huge-NWU Scholarships: Full tuition, fees, room and board over four years.

Requirements: Have a cumulative high school GPA of 3.75 or higher (4.0 scale) | Hold an ACT >27 or SAT >1260.

Application Deadline: December 1

Application link: https://www.nebrwesleyan.edu/admissions/financial-aid-office/undergraduate-aid/first-year-scholarships/huge-nwu-scholarship

NEVADA

1. University of Nevada

Location: Las Vegas, Nevada
Setting: Urban (358 Acres)
Undergraduate Enrollment: 25,862
Type: Public

Army ROTC Scholarship: Awards full tuition plus mandatory fees or applied toward room and board, a $1,200 per year book allowance and a tax-free stipend based on academic status during the academic year.

Requirements: Applicant must be a U.S. citizen | Have a minimum high school GPA of 2.5 | Score a minimum of 920 on the SAT or a 19 composite on the ACT, not including the written portion of the test.

Application Deadline: January 10

Application link:
https://www.unlv.edu/rotc/finaid

2. Nevada State College

Location: Henderson, Nevada
Setting: Urban (510 Acres)
Undergraduate Enrollment: 5,531
Type: Public

Nevada's Otto Huth Scholarship: Award covers tuition, on-campus housing, meal plans, and textbooks for up to $40,000 total.

P.S: It's intended for **youth who've aged out of foster system** and wish to attend an accredited two-year trade school or four-year university.

Requirements: Applicant must Apply before their 20th birthday | Attend a school in Nevada | Begin their post high school education within 12 months of being awarded the scholarship | Have a minimum GPA of 2.0 and plan on attending school full time.

Application Deadline: April 15

Application link:
https://nsc.edu/cedi/scholarships/

NEW HAMPSHIRE

1 University of New Hampshire

Location: Durham, New Hampshire
Setting: Suburban (2,600 Acres)
Undergraduate Enrollment: 11,747
Type: Public

Army ROTC Scholarship: Awards full tuition and fees; grant funds toward room and board; annual book benefit of $1,200; monthly tax-free stipend.

Requirements: Top applicants.

Air Force ROTC Scholarship: Awards full tuition and most lab fees; a textbook allowance; monthly cash stipend.

Application Deadline: November 15
Application link: https://www.unh.edu/financialaid/types-aid/scholarships

NEW JERSEY

1. New Jersey Institute of Technology

Location: Newark, New Jersey
Setting: Urban (48 Acres)
Undergraduate Enrollment: 9,084
Type: Public

National Merit Scholarship: Awards full tuition and fees to students who have been selected by the National Merit Scholarship Corporation (NMSC)

Requirements: To enter the competition, applicant must be either a U.S. citizen or a U.S. lawful permanent resident.

Application Deadline: September 30

Application link: https://www.njit.edu/financialaid/merit-based-scholarships

2. Saint Elizabeth University

Location: Morris Township, New Jersey
Setting: Suburban (200 Acres)
Undergraduate Enrollment: 786
Type: Private

College of Saint Elizabeth International Scholarships: Awards full tuition, room & board, and fees to *international students*.

Requirements: Applicant must have a TOEFL score of at least 173 (computer based), SAT 1200 and an outstanding academic record.

P.S: Only students applying to the Women's College division of the College of Saint Elizabeth are eligible.

Application Deadline: March 1

Application link: https://www.internationalscholarships.com/scholarships/543/College_of_Saint_Elizabeth_International_Scholarships

3. Kean University

Location: Union, New Jersey
Setting: Urban (240 Arces)
Undergraduate Enrollment: 11,686
Type: Public

William Livingston Full Scholarship: Awards up to $50,000. This covers the total cost of attendance.

Requirements: Top Applicants.

Application Deadline: January 1

Application link: https://www.kean.edu/offices/financial-aid/scholarship-services/merit-scholarships-new-incoming-students

NEW MEXICO

1. Eastern New Mexico University

Location: Portales, New Mexico
Setting: Rural (360 Acres)
Undergraduate Enrollment: 4,465
Type: Public

In-State Freshman Scholarship

Green and Silver Presidential Scholarship:

Awards Full tuition, fees and residence hall charges plus $1500 per semester.

Requirements: Applicant must be a New Mexico resident | Be a New Mexico high school graduate, New Mexico General Education Development (GED) recipient, or New Mexico High School Equivalency Test (HiSET) recipient | A minimum 3.0 high school GPA | ACT composite score of 27 (or 1260 – 1290 SAT Evidence – Based Reading and Writing, Math) **OR** 3.5 GPA and ACT composite of 25 (or 1200 – 1220 SAT Evidence – Based Reading and Writing, Math)

Application Deadline: March 1

Application link: https://www.enmu.edu/admission/scholarships

2. University of New Mexico

Location: Albuquerque, New Mexico
Setting: Urban (769 Arces)
Undergraduate Enrollment: 16,124
Type: Public

Freshman New Mexico Resident Scholarships:

Regents' Scholarship: Award approximately $20,000 per year – covers base tuition, fees, and housing.

Requirements: A minimum 3.90 cumulative high school GPA.

National Merit Finalist Scholarship: Award approximately $20,000 per year – covers base tuition, fees, and housing.

Requirements: Awarded National Merit Finalist.

Application Deadline: December 1

Application link: https://scholarship.unm.edu/

NEW MEXICO

3. New Mexico Highlands University

Location: Las Vegas, New Mexico
Setting: Rural (175 Arces)
Undergraduate Enrollment: 1,797
Type: Public

Debt Free Four Year Education: Highlands University offers Debt-Free-Four-Year Education to Students from partner High Schools (Santa Fe Public Schools, Denver Public Schools, and most of the schools in the Northeast Regional Education Cooperative, including Mora, Santa Rosa, Wagon Mound, West Las Vegas, and Las Vegas City school districts

Requirements: A minimum 3.0 high school GPA.

Regent's New Mexico scholars Scholarship: Awards full tuition and fees plus $500 per semester.

Eligibility: Applicant must rank in the top 5 percent of graduating class or 25 ACT, family income of $60,000 or less.

Application Deadline: March 1
Application link: https://www.nmhu.edu/financial-aid-2/scholarships/

NEW YORK

1. University of Rochester

Location: Rochester, New York
Setting: Urban (707 Acres)
Undergraduate Enrollment: 6,521
Type: Private

Alan and Jane Handler Endowed scholarship:

Handler students will receive assured, complete financial support (tuition, fees, room, board, books, personal expenses and transportation), plus $5,000 in guaranteed funding to support academic or professional enrichment as well as individual and group opportunities, for the duration of the regular four year academic program.

Requirements: Top applicants.

Application link: https://admissions.rochester.edu/handler-scholarship/

2. Alfred University

Location: Alfred, New York
Setting: Rural (600 Acres)
Undergraduate Enrollment: 1,594
Type: Private

Army ROTC Scholarships: This scholarship provides full financial assistance (full tuition, mandatory fees or can be used for room and board expenses of $10,000 per school year, plus a tax free subsistence allowance for up to 10 months of $420 per month and $1,200 annually for textbooks, classroom supplies and equipment.

Application link: https://www.alfred.edu/student-life/military-affairs/grants-financial-aid.cfm

NEW YORK

Fordham University

Location: New York City, New York
Setting: Urban (93 Acres)
Undergraduate Enrollment: 9,399
Type: Private

Cunniffe Presidential Scholarship: Award covers tuition, room, board, and fees. It is renewable for 4 years. Recipients are also eligible for a maximum of $20,000 over four years to use for academic enrichment experiences.

Requirements: Check site for more details.

Application Deadline: November 1

Application link: https://www.fordham.edu/undergraduate-admission/apply/scholarships-and-grants/

Canisius College

Location: Buffalo, New York
Setting: Urban (72 Acres)
Undergraduate Enrollment: 2,213
Type: Private

Army ROTC:

The Army ROTC Scholarship can be used for either full tuition & fees, or as room and board scholarship. It provides a book stipend, and a subsistence (living allowance) while enrolled in college.

Application Deadline: January 10

Application link: https://www.canisius.edu/admissions/scholarships-tuition-aid/scholarships-financial-aid/scholarships/freshmen-scholarships

Adelphi University

Location: Garden City, New York
Setting: Suburban (75 Acres)
Undergraduate Enrollment: 5,124
Type: Private

Athletic Grants: Awards up to Full tuition, fees, room and board.

Requirements: Applicants athletic performance/record | Top applicants.

Application Deadline: October 1

Application link: https://www.adelphi.edu/aid/scholarships/institutional/additional-awards/

NEW YORK

6. Oswego State University of New York

Location: Oswego, New York
Setting: Rural (700 Acres)
Undergraduate Enrollment: 6,673
Type: Public

Possibility Scholars Program: Award when combined with existing need-based aid covers the total cost of attendance.

P.S: New York state students entering STEM fields (Science, Technology, Engineering or Math) are eligible for consideration, with priority given to high-achieving students with significant financial need.

Requirements: Student should exhibit a high degree of excellence.

Application Deadline: November 15

Application link: https://www.oswego.edu/financial-aid/scholarships

7. Roberts Wesleyan College

Location: Rochester, New York
Setting: Suburban (188 Acres)
Undergraduate Enrollment: 1,197
Type: Private

The Max and Marian Farash Charitable Foundation's First in the Family Scholarship Program: Award covers all additional funds needed to *completely pay* for the Farash Scholar's tuition, room and board, textbooks, and mandatory fees.

Eligibility: Freshman from Monroe or Ontario County (New York) who will be the first in his/her family (parents, step-parents, or siblings) to have attended any college/university.

Application Deadline: February 14

Application link: https://www.roberts.edu/undergraduate/tuition-and-aid/grants-scholarships/merit-scholarships/farash-scholarship/

NEW YORK

Syracuse University

Location: Syracuse, New York
Setting: City (721 Arces)
Undergraduate Enrollment: 14,479
Type: Private

Haudenosaunee Promise Scholarship: Award covers tuition, housing and meals (on campus, up to the amount allotted through the cost of attendance) and mandatory fees.

Eligibility: Applicant must be a certified citizen of one of the historic Haudenosaunee nations (Mohawk, Oneida, Onondaga, Cayuga, Seneca, or Tuscarora) | Have resided on one of the Haudenosaunee nation territories listed for a minimum of four years prior to and during their enrollment at Syracuse University.

Requirements: Top applicants

Check site for eligible *Haudenosaunee Territories…*

Application Deadline: November 15

Application link: https://financialaid.syr.edu/scholarships/su/

Pratt Institute

Location: Brooklyn, New York
Setting: Urban (25 Acres)
Undergraduate Enrollment: 2,927
Type: Private

President's Wallace Augustus Rayfield Scholarship: Awards Full ride scholarships *(to students from New York City and New York State)*

Eligibility: Awarded to students in five degree-granting schools of Architecture, Art, Design, Information, Liberal Arts and Sciences.

Requirements: Top applicants

Kathryn and Kenneth Chenault Scholarship: Awards tuition, room and board, fees, books and supplies.

P.S: This Scholarship is established to support *diversity in the school of Architecture*.

Requirements: Top applicants

Balenciaga and The Black Alumni of Pratt: Award covers full undergraduate attendance – including tuition, fees, room and board, books and supplies.

Eligibility: Awarded to students in the School of Design, School of Art, and School of Architecture.

P.S: This Scholarship will support diversity within these schools and their professional fields.

Requirements: Top applicants

Application Deadline: November 1

Application link: https://catalog.pratt.edu/undergraduate/financial-aid/scholarships/

NORTH CAROLINA

1. Gardner Webb University

Location: Boiling Springs, North Carolina
Setting: Rural (240 Acres)
Undergraduate Enrollment: 1,999
Type: Private

The Tucker Heart, Soul, Mind, and Strength Scholarship: Full tuition, room and board.

Requirements: Ministers, teachers and community leaders can nominate a worthy student for a chance at this top scholarship.

Application Deadline: Nominations should be submitted before the end of October.

The Andrews Scholarship: Award covers Full tuition, room and board, and $800 per year for books.

Requirements: Top applicants | Applicant Must have demonstrated financial need | Must be a first generation college student | Must have a demonstrated commitment to diversity | Must be a *male* | Must *not* be a student athlete.

Application Deadline: April 1

Application link: https://gardner-webb.edu/admissions-aid/scholarships-and-grants/

2. Elizabeth City State University

Location: Elizabeth City, North Carolina
Setting: Rural (154 Acres)
Undergraduate Enrollment: 1,910
Type: Public

Chancellor's Academic Scholarship: A fully funded four year scholarship (full tuition, student fees, university housing, meals and textbooks.)

Requirements: Applicant must be a U.S. citizen or a permanent resident | Have a minimum 3.5 unweighted cumulative GPA.

Application Deadline: January 15

Application link: https://www.ecsu.edu/academics/enrollment-management-retention/financial-aid/scholarships.html

NORTH CAROLINA

3. North Carolina A & T

Location: Greensboro, North Carolina
Setting: Urban (800 Acres)
Undergraduate Enrollment: 11,130
Type: Public

National Alumni Scholarship: Full tuition, related fees, room & board.

Eligibility: Applicant must be a U.S. citizen | A minimum 3.5 GPA (4.0 scale) | ACT and SAT score are optional for the 2021-2022 year.

Lewis and Elizabeth Dowdy Scholarship: Full tuition, related fees, room & board.

Eligibility: A minimum 3.75 cumulative GPA (weighted) | Minimum SAT score of 1270 or 27 ACT (test optional for the 2021 applicants) | Applicant must be a U.S. citizen or eligible non-citizen.

Application Deadline: December 15
Application link:
https://www.ncat.edu/admissions/financial-aid/types-of-aid/scholarships/freshmen-scholarships.php

4. Wake Forest University

Location: Winston-Salem, North Carolina
Setting: Suburban (340 Acres)
Undergraduate Enrollment: 5,441
Type: Private

Guy T. Carswell Scholarship: Full tuition, fees, room and board, and includes an allowance for books and personal expenses. Scholars may receive up to $5,000 at least one summer for approved travel or study projects.

Requirements: Top Applicants

Joseph G. Gordon Scholarship: Full tuition, fees, room and board, and includes an allowance for books and personal expenses. Scholars may receive up to $5,000 at least one summer for approved travel or study projects.

Leadership and Character Scholarship: Full tuition, fees, room and board, and includes an allowance for books and personal expenses.

Graylyn Scholarship: Full tuition, room and board, plus $3,400 for personal expenses.

Requirements: Top Applicants.

Nancy Susan Reynolds Scholarship: Full tuition, room and board, plus $3,400 for personal expenses.

Requirements: Top Applicants.

P.S: Scholars are encouraged to apply for up to $5,000 for a research, study, or travel project during each of the three summers between the first and senior years.

Application Deadline: November 15
Application link: https://financialaid.wfu.edu/merit#scholarships

NORTH CAROLINA

5. UNC, Chapel Hill

Location: Chapel Hill, North Carolina
Setting: Suburban (729 Acres)
Undergraduate Enrollment: 19,399
Type: Public

Kenan Music Scholarship: This generous scholarship offers the opportunity to combine musical studies with coursework (or a second major) and a four year, full-tuition scholarship (including student fees, room & board).

Requirements: Interested students must submit a scholarship audition request directly to the Department of Music to be considered for this opportunity.

Reserve Office Training Corps (ROTC) Scholarship: Awards full tuition and fees, a $600 per-semester book allowance, and a monthly stipend between $300 and $500, depending on the student's year at the University. Upon graduation, cadets may become officers in the active Army or remain in the Army Reserve.

Application Deadline: March 1

Application link: https://studentaid.unc.edu/incoming/what-aid-is-available/scholarships/

6. Davidson College

Location: Davidson, North Carolina
Setting: Suburban (665 Acres)
Undergraduate Enrollment: 1,983
Type: Private

Nomination Scholarships:

You must be nominated for consideration.

John M. Belk Scholarship: Full tuition, fees, room and board plus special study stipends that allow you great flexibility in the on and off-campus opportunities you choose to explore.

Lowell L. Bryan Scholarship: Full tuition and fees.

Requirements: Applicant must be a Scholar athlete.

Charles Scholarship: Full tuition, fees, room and board, Book and personal expense allowance, Travel allowance (three roundtrips to Chicago), A new laptop once during a scholar's Davidson career, Special study opportunity funds.

Competition Scholarships:

William Holt Terry Scholarship: Full tuition and fees annually, and a one-time $3,000 special opportunity stipend.

There are lot's of full ride scholarship opportunities available at the Davidson College.

Application Deadline: December 1

Application link: https://www.davidson.edu/admission-and-financial-aid/financial-aid/scholarships

NORTH CAROLINA

7. Salem College

Location: Winston-Salem, North Carolina
Setting: City (57 Acres)
Undergraduate Enrollment: 492
Type: Private

Salem College Promise: Full tuition and fees.

Eligibility: Applicant must be a North Carolina resident | Pell-eligible, with an estimated family contribution of $0-$5,000 (per FASFA)

Outstanding applicants may receive scholarships covering the full cost of attendance through named awards. Check site for more details.

Application Deadline: November 1

Application link: https://www.salem.edu/admissions/scholarships

8. University of North Carolina - Greensboro

Location: Greensboro, North Carolina
Setting: Urban (266 Acres)
Undergraduate Enrollment: 15,995
Type: Public

Blue & Gold Scholarships: Full tuition, fees, room and board.

Eligibility: Academically talented incoming freshmen.

Application Deadline: December 1

Application link: https://admissions.uncg.edu/costs-aid/scholarships/

9. Saint Augustine's University

Location: Raleigh, North Carolina
Setting: Urban (122 Acres)
Undergraduate Enrollment: 1,110
Type: Private

Presidential Scholarship: Awards a full direct cost of attendance.

Requirements: High School GPA of 3.8 or higher | A minimum 1100 SAT score or a 22 ACT score.

Application Deadline: May 3

Application link: https://www.st-aug.edu/cost-aid/financial-aid/scholarship/

NORTH CAROLINA

10 Duke University

Location: Durham, North Carolina
Setting: Suburban (8,600+ Acres)
Undergraduate Enrollment: 6,717
Type: Private

Duke University gives out a number of prominent full-ride merit scholarships, including the Benjamin N. Duke (B.N.) Scholars, Angier B. Duke (A.B.) Scholars, David M. Rubenstein Scholars, Reginaldo Howard Memorial Scholars, Trinity Scholars, University Scholars, Robertson Scholars, etc. These scholarships give full monetary assistance to the recipients, typically in addition to programmatic resources and professional assistance.

Karsh Intentional Scholarship: Full tuition, mandatory fees, room and board, plus generous funding for domestic and international summer experiences, etc.

Eligibility: Top **International** undergraduate applicants.

Application Deadline: February 1

Application link: https://medschool.duke.edu/education/health-professions-education-programs/doctor-medicine-md-program/curriculum/third-year-45

11 North Carolina State University

Location: Raleigh, North Carolina
Setting: City (2,137 Acres)
Undergraduate Enrollment: 26,150
Type: Public

Park Scholarship: A fully funded four year scholarship (full tuition, fees, room and board, books and supplies, travel, personal expenses and lot's more.)

Requirements: Top scholars in the applicant pool

Application Deadline: November 1

Application link: https://giving.ncsu.edu/where-to-give/scholarships/

NORTH CAROLINA

12 North Carolina Wesleyan College

Location: Rocky Mount, North Carolina
Setting: Suburban (200 Acres)
Undergraduate Enrollment: 1,603
Type: Private

John & Charles Wesley Heritage Scholarship: Full tuition, room (double only), board & books.

Requirements: 4.0 weighted GPA / 3.75 unweighted | 1240 SAT / 26 ACT.

Application link: https://ncwc.edu/scholarships/

13 Lees-McRae College

Location: Banner Elk, North Carolina
Setting: Rural (460 Acres)
Undergraduate Enrollment: 836
Type: Private

Shelton Scholarship: Awards Full tuition, room and board for four years.

Requirements: A minimum 3.75 high school GPA | 1150 SAT score (or ACT equivalent)

Application Deadline: December 1

Application link: https://www.lmc.edu/admissions/financial-aid/types-of-aid.htm

NORTH CAROLINA

14 Appalachian State University

Location: Boone, North Carolina
Setting: Rural (500 Acres)
Undergraduate Enrollment: 18,061
Type: Public

Chancellor's Scholarship: Award covers full institutional costs for up to 4 years; including tuition and fees, room and board, book rental, plus study abroad opportunities, numerous classroom and experiential research opportunities and academic mentoring in the living–learning community of the Honors College.

P.S: Recipients must be accepted into the Honors College.

Requirements: Top students in the applicants pool.

Murray Family ACCESS Scholarship Program: Awards Full tuition, fees, room and board and book rental.

P.S: The Murray Family Appalachian Commitment to a College Education for Student Success (ACCESS) Scholarship Program ensures 50 students from low-income families in North Carolina can attend Appalachian debt-free.

Requirements: Students must demonstrate or have a track record of being excellent.

15 East Carolina University

Location: Greenville, North Carolina
Setting: City (1,600 Acres)
Undergraduate Enrollment: 23,056
Type: Public

EC Scholars Program: Award covers in-state tuition for eight continuous semesters, Living arrangements Ballard Residence Hall, the newest residence on campus located on College Hill, Priority course registration to guarantee your needed classes and preferred times, $5,000 stipend to support a required Study Abroad experience, and a lot of other benefits.

Requirements: Top scholars in the applicants pool

Application Deadline: October 1
Application link: https://ecscholars.ecu.edu/

Application Deadline: November 15
Application link:
https://scholarships.appstate.edu/first-year-students/signature-scholarships

NORTH CAROLINA

16 University of North Carolina, Charlotte

Location: Charlotte, North Carolina
Setting: Urban (1,000 Acres)
Undergraduate Enrollment: 24,175
Type: Public

Albert Engineering Leadership Scholars Program: Award covers –

- ✓ An annual renewable merit scholarship, including tuition, fees, room and board ($21,500 a year)
- ✓ Membership in the University Honors Program
- ✓ Automatic acceptance into the Engineering Leadership Academy
- ✓ A $6,000 stipend to support housing and meals during a summer internship
- ✓ A $2,500 stipend for study abroad
- ✓ A Laptop or comparable technology purchase
- ✓ Research and Professional development opportunities, and lots more…

17 Meredith College

Location: Raleigh, North Carolina
Setting: Urban (225 Acres)
Undergraduate Enrollment: 1,521
Type: Private

Meredith Legacy Scholarship: Awards Full tuition, on campus room and board, college-wide fees (four academic years), books, supplies, international study, and other academic enrichment programs.

Requirements: An average SAT/ACT 1510/34 | Weighted GPA of 4.65, demonstrated leadership and service to others.

Application Deadline: January 15

Application link: https://www.meredith.edu/financial-assistance/financial-assistance-undergraduate-scholarships/

Requirements: An unweighted high school GPA of 3.50 – 4.00 or Weighted high school GPA of 3.80 – 5.00 | SAT 1320/1600 or ACT 28/36 | Applicants must be U.S. citizens or permanent residents | Applicants are expected to submit a list of activities, two academic letters of recommendation, one leadership recommendation, and two thoughtfully considered essays.

Application Deadline: November 1

Application link: https://honorscollege.charlotte.edu/albertscholars.uncc.edu

NORTH DAKOTA

1. University of North Dakota

Location: Grand Forks, North Dakota
Setting: City (521 Arces)
Undergraduate Enrollment: 9,796
Type: Public

National Merit Scholars

This scholarship is awarded to National Merit Scholar Finalist or Semi-Finalist from North Dakota or Minnesota.

Awards Full tuition and mandatory student fees. This scholarship is in addition to other UND scholarships and waivers you're eligible to receive (up to the full cost of attendance)

Requirements: National Merit Finalist/Semi-Finalist | Applicant must select UND as first choice on the National merit application.

Application Deadline: December 15

Application link: https://und.edu/one-stop/financial-aid/scholarships.html

OHIO

1. Ohio State University

Location: Columbus, Ohio
Setting: Urban (1,665 Acres)
Undergraduate Enrollment: 46,984
Type: Public

Land Grant Opportunity Scholarship: Award covers the full cost of attendance. This scholarship is awarded to students who are Pell-eligible and demonstrate academic merit.

Eligibility: Applicant MUST be an Ohio resident.

Eminence Fellows Program and Scholarship: Awards up to full cost of attendance, plus an enrichment grant valued at $3,000 accessible after the first year of successful study.

Criteria: Only U.S. citizens and permanent residents are eligible to apply | Finalist are selected based on the strength of their Common Application.

Morrill Scholarship Program

Awards Levels: *Distinction* (the value of the cost of attendance)

Requirements: Top Applicants.

Application Deadline: December 1

Application link:
http://undergrad.osu.edu/cost-and-aid/merit-based-scholarships

2. University of Cincinnati

Location: Cincinnati, Ohio
Setting: Urban (253 Acres)
Undergraduate Enrollment: 28,657
Type: Public

Cincinnatus Scholarship Program: Ranges from $1,500 annually up to full tuition, room and board, and a book allowance.

Requirements: Qualifying students will be determined based on their overall admission application.

Marian Spencer Scholarship: Awards Full tuition, room and board, and a book allowance.

P.S: Specifically reserved for CPS students in the top 10% of their senior class.

Requirements: This scholarship is awarded to top 10% students in each Cincinnati public school (CPS) who exemplify the spirit of Spencer.

Application Deadline: December 1

Application link:
https://www.uc.edu/about/financial-aid/aid/scholarships.html

OHIO

3 Miami University

Location: Oxford, Ohio
Setting: Rural (2,100 Acres)
Undergraduate Enrollment: 16,522
Type: Public

Presidential Fellows Program: Full tuition & fees, room and board, plus a one-time $5,000 academic enrichment stipend.

Requirements: Top scholars.

Application Deadline: December 1

Application link: https://miamioh.edu/academics/honors-programs/presidential-fellows/

4 Cleveland State University

Location: Cleveland, Ohio
Setting: Urban (85 Arces)
Undergraduate Enrollment: 11,245
Type: Public

Honors Program: Full tuition and fees.

Requirements: A minimum ACT composite score of 30 OR SAT score of 1380 | Rank in the top 10% of high school class.

Jack, Joseph and Morton Mandel Honors College

Awards full tuition scholarship at the in-state tuition rate and other associated fees.

Eligibility: International Student's.

Sullivan-Deckard and Helen Packer Scholarship: Award covers Financial aid for tuition, books, fees, and instructional resources. Year – round housing with an approved meal plan. Academic coaching and institutional support services plus a lot of other benefits.

Eligibility: This Scholarship is *designed for youth who are aging out of foster care or experienced foster care* and aspire to pursue an undergraduate degree.

Application Deadline: January 15

Application link: https://www.csuohio.edu/financial-aid/new-incoming-freshman

OHIO

5. University of Toledo

Location: Toledo, Ohio
Setting: Urban (1,037 Acres)
Undergraduate Enrollment: 14,406
Type: Public

Presidential Scholarship: Full tuition, room and board, general fee, a one-time $3,000 stipend for a summer experience.

Requirements: Minimum high school cumulative GPA of 3.8 | 30 ACT or 1360 SAT.

Application Deadline: December 1

Application link:
https://www.utoledo.edu/admission/freshman/tuition/

6. University of Mount Union

Location: Alliance, Ohio
Setting: City (123 Acres)
Undergraduate Enrollment: 1,958
Type: Private

ROTC Scholarship:

Air Force and Army ROTC Scholarship:

Awards Full tuition, free on-campus housing and board.

Requirements: Top Applicants in the applicants pool.

Check site for more details…

Application Deadline: November 8

Application link:
https://www.mountunion.edu/scholarships-and-grants

OHIO

7. Case Western Reserve University

Location: Cleveland, Ohio
Setting: Urban (267 Arces)
Undergraduate Enrollment: 5,433
Type: Private

Joan C. Edwards Scholarship: Awards full tuition, room, board, fees, books and personal expenses, as well as conditional admission to the Case Western Reserve University School of Medicine; a medical school scholarship in the amount of tuition and a $20,000 per year stipend!

Criteria: This scholarship is awarded to students in the Cleveland Metropolitan School District with an interest in becoming a physician.

The Army & Air Force ROTC Program also provides significant college scholarships that cover tuition, books, fees, and monthly stipends for those that compete for the opportunity.

Application Deadline: January 15

Application link: https://case.edu/admission/tuition-aid/scholarships

8. Marietta College

Location: Marietta, Ohio
Setting: Suburban (90 Arces)
Undergraduate Enrollment: 1,168
Type: Private

John G. McCoy Scholarship: Awards Full tuition, fees, standard room and board.

Requirements: Top scholars in the applicants pool.

Application Deadline: February 15

Application link: https://www.marietta.edu/scholarships

OKLAHOMA

1. Langston University

Location: Langston, Oklahoma
Setting: Rural (40 Acres)
Undergraduate Enrollment: 2,026
Type: Public

1890 USDA Scholar Program: Full tuition, room and board. Requirements: Top applicants

McCabe Scholarship: The McCabe Scholarship covers the costs of tuition, fees, room and board (designated campus housing only), and $500 per semester for books.

Regents' Scholarship: Covers the costs of room and board in campus housing only.

N.B: This scholarships goes out by e-mail invitation only to students with good academic records.

Application Deadline: May 15

Application link: https://www.langston.edu/langston-university-scholarships

2. University of Oklahoma

Location: Norman, Oklahoma
Setting: City (3,326 Acres)
Undergraduate Enrollment: 21,383
Type: Public

National Merit Finalist Scholarship: Awards $68,500 to Resident Freshmen and $121,500 to Non-resident applicant's. This amount covers the total cost of attendance for undergraduate studies at the University of Oklahoma.

Criteria: National Merit Finalist.

Military Scholarships are also available for incoming students.

Application Deadline: December 15

Application link: https://www.ou.edu/admissions/affordability/scholarships#intlfreshman

OKLAHOMA

3. Oklahoma Christian University

Location: Edmond, Oklahoma
Setting: City (200 Acres)
Undergraduate Enrollment: 1,698
Type: Private

National Merit Scholar Award

Award amount: OC award + federal grants + state grants + National Merit Award finalist = up to 17 credit hours per semester of full tuition, mandatory fees, cost of room and meal plan.

Requirements: Applicant must select OC as your first-choice university to the National Merit Corporation.

Application Deadline: December 1

Application link: https://www.oc.edu/admissions/financial-services/scholarships

4. Cameron University

Location: Lawton, Oklahoma
Setting: City (160 Acres)
Undergraduate Enrollment: 3,459
Type: Public

The Incoming freshmen PLUS scholarship: The scholarship will provide recipients with a full tuition waiver for up to 18 hours per semester, a room waiver to cover the scholar's portion of a double room in Shepler Center, and a $400 stipend per semester.

Requirements: Applicant must be a resident of Oklahoma | A minimum high school GPA of 3.0 (unweighted) OR 2.8 and be in the top 25% of the graduating senior class | Achieve ACT minimum composite score of 20 (or SAT equivalent)

Application Deadline: February 3

Application link: https://www.cameron.edu/plus/incoming-freshman-plus-scholarship

OKLAHOMA

5

Oklahoma City University

Location: Oklahoma City, Oklahoma
Setting: Urban (104 Arces)
Undergraduate Enrollment: 1,526
Type: Private

Clara Luper Scholarship: Block tuition, standard room & board, and membership in the prestigious President's Leadership Class.

Requirements: Top Applicants | High school GPA of 3.0 or higher.

American Indian Scholarship: Block tuition, standard room & board, and membership in the prestigious President's Leadership Class.

Requirements: Top applicants | High school GPA of 3.0 or higher.

The Mary Ellen & George R. Randall Endowed Great Plan Scholarship for Pre-Med and Science: Full tuition, basic room & board, and fees.

This Scholarship is awarded to a graduating high school senior who plans to study pre-medicine at OCU

Criteria: Study pre-medicine or science.

Application Deadline: February 1

Application link: https://www.okcu.edu/financialaid/types-of-assistance/scholarships/freshmen

OREGON

University of Oregon

Location: Eugene, Oregon
Setting: City (295 Acres)
Undergraduate Enrollment: 18,045
Type: Public

Stamps Scholarships

Oregon resident Stamps Scholars receive UO resident tuition, fees, room, and board for four years of undergraduate study. *Out-of-state* recipients receive non-resident tuition and fees. All recipients benefit from up to $12,000 in enrichment funds to be used over four years to help pursue study abroad, unpaid internships, or other experiences.

Requirements: A minimum 3.85 cumulative high school grade point average on a 4.0 scale | A minimum 1300 SAT or 28 ACT (no test scores required for Fall 2021 Applicant)

Application Deadline: November 16

Application link: https://financialaid.uoregon.edu/stamps_scholarship

PENNSYLVANIA

1. Villanova University

Location: Villanova, Pennsylvania
Setting: Suburban (260 Acres)
Undergraduate Enrollment: 7,037
Type: Private

Presidential Scholarship: Full tuition, room, board (up to 21 meals per week plan), general fee, and the cost of textbooks for eight consecutive semesters.

Criteria: In order to be considered for the Presidential scholarship, students must first be nominated by the chief academic officer of their high school (principal, president, headmaster), secondary school counselor, or an official school designee.

St. Martin de Porres Scholarship: Full tuition and general fees.

Eligibility: U.S. citizens or permanent residents from one or more of the most underrepresented groups at the Villanova University.

Anthony Randazzo Endowed Presidential Scholarship: Full tuition, room, board (up to 21 meals per week plan), general fee, and the cost of textbooks for eight consecutive semesters.

Eligibility: Awarded to a first year African American/Black student | Applicant must reside in the city of Philadelphia, Pennsylvania.

Application Deadline: January 2
Application link:
https://www1.villanova.edu/university/undergraduate-admission/Financial-Assistance-and-scholarship/merit-based-scholarships.html

2. Elizabethtown College

Location: Elizabethtown, Pennsylvania
Setting: Suburban (203 Acres)
Undergraduate Enrollment: 1,688
Type: Private

Stamps Scholarship: Award covers full tuition as well as an enrichment fund which is funded by the Strive Foundation and Elizabethtown College.

Requirements: Top students.

Application Deadline: January 15
Application link:
https://www.etown.edu/admissions/financial-aid/index.aspx

PENNSYLVANIA

3 Saint Vincent College

Location: Latrobe, Pennsylvania
Setting: Suburban (200 Acres)
Undergraduate Enrollment: 1,462
Type: Private

Wimmer Scholarship Competition: Awards Full tuition, room and board.

Requirements: A minimum cumulative high school GPA of 3.75 | SAT (ERW and Math) score of 1300 or above, a minimum ACT score of 28 or a CLT of 86.

Application Deadline: March 1

Application link: https://www.stvincent.edu/admission-aid/undergraduate-students.html

4 Temple University

Location: Philadelphia, Pennsylvania
Setting: Urban (406 Acres)
Undergraduate Enrollment: 27,306
Type: Public

Athletic Scholarships: Awards Full and partial tuition scholarships plus room and board and book allowances.

Eligibility: Participants in all varsity sports will be considered for scholarships.

P.S: Army ROTC and Air Force ROTC Scholarships are also available.

Application Deadline: February 1

Application link: https://sfs.temple.edu/financial-aid-types/scholarships/new-incoming-students/

PENNSYLVANIA

5 University of Pittsburgh

Location: Pittsburgh, Pennsylvania
Setting: Urban (145 Acres)
Undergraduate Enrollment: 19,197
Type: Public

Chancellor's Scholarship: Awards Full tuition, mandatory fees, average room and board plan, Guaranteed Pitt Honors housing.

Eligibility: Applicant must be a U.S. Citizen or Permanent resident.

Requirements: Top scholar in applicants pool.

Stamps Scholarship: Awards Full tuition, mandatory fees, room and board plus an allowance for books and supplies, transportation expenses, and personal costs, Access to an enrichment fund of up to $17,400 to be used over four years for the purpose of global experiences, unpaid internships, leadership training, research, and other academic experiences.

Eligibility: *Pennsylvania residency* | Applicant must be a U.S. Citizen or Permanent resident.

Application Deadline: December 1

Application link: https://financialaid.pitt.edu/types-of-aid/scholarships/

6 Susquehanna University

Location: Selinsgrove, Pennsylvania
Setting: Rural (325 Acres)
Undergraduate Enrollment: 2,323
Type: Private

Reserve Officers' Training Corps (ROTC): Awards Full tuition, room (double only) and board.

Eligibility: Cadets of the Bison Battalion Army ROTC

Application Deadline: December 1

Application link: https://www.susqu.edu/admission-and-aid/tuition-and-financial-aid/financial-aid-options/scholarships/

PENNSYLVANIA

7. Waynesburg University

Location: Waynesburg, Pennsylvania
Setting: Rural (30 Acres)
Undergraduate Enrollment: 1,257
Type: Private

Founders Scholarship: A full tuition and fees scholarship for Pennsylvania residents.

Requirements: Resident of the state of Pennsylvania | High school cumulative GPA of a 3.5 or higher | SAT of 1200 or higher on Evidence-Based Reading & Writing and Math or ACT composite score of 26 or higher.

Application Deadline: January 8

Application link: https://www.waynesburg.edu/admissions/scholarships-and-awards

8. Lincoln University

Location: Oxford, Pennsylvania
Setting: Rural (422 Acres)
Undergraduate Enrollment: 1,895
Type: Public

Merit Scholarship: Awards Full tuition & General fees.

Eligibility: International Student's | Minimum GPA: 3.30 cumulative | Minimum Test Score: 1020 SAT / 20 ACT (composite)

Application Deadline: February 1

Application link: https://www.lincoln.edu/admissions/office-undergraduate-admissions/scholarships

9. Albright College

Location: Reading, Pennsylvania
Setting: Suburban (118 Acres)
Undergraduate Enrollment: 1,537
Type: Private

Warren L. Davis Scholarship: Awards Full tuition, room and board.

Requirements: Top applicants.

P.S: Students who are invited to apply must submit a prompted essay as well as a character recommendation

Application Deadline: December 15

Application link: https://www.albright.edu/admission-aid/scholarships/

RHODE ISLAND

1. Providence College

Location: Providence, Rhode Island
Setting: City (105 Acres)
Undergraduate Enrollment: 4,298
Type: Private

Roddy Scholarship: Awards Full tuition, fees, room and board.

Requirements: Applicants must aspire to a career in the medical profession | Consideration is based on outstanding academic achievement in high school | Awarded to first-year students who reside in the United States.

Application Deadline: November 1

Application link: https://financial-aid.providence.edu/types-of-assistance/institutional-merit-based/

2. University of Rhode Island

Location: South Kingstown, Rhode Island
Settting: Rural (1,245 Acres)
Undergraduate Enrollment: 14,073
Type: Public

Thomas M. Ryan Scholars Program: Awards Full tuition, fees, housing, dining, books, and one Global winter travel J term experience with faculty.

Requirements: Top Applicants.

Alfred J. Verrecchia Business Scholars Program: Awards Full tuition, fees, housing, dining, books, and one Global winter travel J term experience with faculty.

Requirements: Awarded to selected students interested in majoring in Business.

Application Deadline: June 26

Application link: https://web.uri.edu/admission/scholarships/

SOUTH CAROLINA

1. Presbyterian College

Location: Clinton, South Carolina
Setting: Rural (240 Acres)
Undergraduate Enrollment: 1,048
Type: Private

Griffith Scholarship: Awards Full tuition, fees, room and board for four years.

Requirements: Top students in applicants pool.

ROTC Scholarships

U.S Army ROTC: Awards Full tuition and fees, $1,200 annually for books, and a monthly stipend for contracted cadets. Presbyterian College may pay room and board for these scholarship recipients.

Requirements: Applicant must be a U.S. citizen | Be between the ages of 17 and 26 | Have a high school GPA of at least 2.50 | Have a high school diploma or equivalent | Score a minimum of 920 on the SAT (math/verbal) or 19 on the ACT (excluding the required writing test scores)

P.S: Applicants must meet physical standards. Check site for more details…

Application Deadline: December 1

Application link: https://www.presby.edu/admissions/tuition-aid/scholarships/

2. South Carolina State University

Location: Orangeburg, South Carolina
Setting: Suburban (160 Acres)
Undergraduate Enrollment: 2,020
Type: Public

Presidential Scholarship: Award covers full tuition, room & board.

Requirements: A minimum GPA of 3.50 | Achieve at least 1200 (CR+M) on the SAT 1 test or 27 on the ACT test.

Application Deadline: This scholarship is awarded based on availability of funds.

Application link: https://www2.scsu.edu/scholarships/institutionalscholarships.aspx

SOUTH CAROLINA

Allen University

Location: Columbia, South Carolina
Setting: City (150 Acres)
Undergraduate Enrollment: 656
Type: Private

Presidential Scholarship: Awards full tuition, room, board, and fees.

Requirements: A minimum GPA of 3.40 | A minimum 1200 SAT or 25 ACT score.

Application Deadline: June 15

Application link: https://allenuniversity.edu/grants-and-scholarships

The Citadel – Military College of South Carolina

Location: Charleston, South Carolina
Setting: Urban (300 Acres)
Undergraduate Enrollment: 2,911
Type: Military

Full Academic Scholarships: Award covers full tuition, room & board plus quartermaster charges.

Requirements: Top Applicants

ROTC Scholarships are also available, check site for more details…

Application Deadline: October 1

Application link: https://go.citadel.edu/financial-aid/scholarships/cadet-scholarships/

SOUTH CAROLINA

5. Furman University

Location: Greenville, South Carolina
Setting: Suburban (800 Acres)
Undergraduate Enrollment: 2,345
Type: Private

James B. Duke Scholarships: Award covers full tuition, room & board and all fees for four years.

Requirements: Top scholars in applicants' pool.

James A. Vaughn Scholarships: Award covers full tuition, room & board and all fees for four years.

Eligibility: Scholarships will be awarded to *new incoming Black or African-American students* who currently reside in the state of South Carolina and have demonstrated outstanding academic achievement and a strong commitment to their communities.

ROTC Scholarships: Awards up to full tuition and fees, plus a monthly stipend during the academic year.

Requirements: Top Applicants

Application Deadline: April 15

Application link: https://www.furman.edu/financial-aid/aid-types/merit-based-scholarships/

6. Limestone University

Location: Gaffney, South Carolina
Setting: Suburban (125 Acres)
Undergraduate Enrollment: 1,818
Type: Private

Presidential Palmetto Scholarship: Award covers Full tuition, fees, room & board.

Requirements: Applicant must be a SC Palmetto Fellows recipient.

Application Deadline: November 15

Application link: https://www.limestone.edu/financial-aid/scholarships-and-grants

SOUTH CAROLINA

7. North Greenville University

Location: Tigerville, South Carolina
Setting: Rural (330 Acres)
Undergraduate Enrollment: 1,993
Type: Private

The Lifeshape Scholarship: Award covers Full tuition, room & board, books/materials (through Slingshot), and required fees.

Requirements: A minimum 3.75 unweighted GPA | 1320 SAT or 28 ACT or 88 CLT

NGU Fellows Scholarship: Awards Full tuition, room & board (*to South Carolina residents*)

Eligibility: South Carolina residents who meet the requirements for the Palmetto Fellows Scholarship will be considered for the NGU Fellows Scholarship.

Application Deadline: October 15

Application link: https://ngu.edu/admissions/financial-aid/undergraduate/

8. Wofford College

Location: Spartanburg, South Carolina
Setting: Urban (170 Acres)
Undergraduate Enrollment: 1,772
Type: Private

Richardson Family Scholarship: Award covers Full tuition, fees, room & board, a monthly stipend for books and miscellaneous expenses, A laptop computer for entering first-year students, Summer internships, with one involving opportunity for overseas travel, A January travel experience.

Criteria for selection: Applicants must be nominated as a Wofford Scholar by their high school guidance counsellors | Moral force of character | Strong family commitment | Instincts to lead | Scholarly accomplishments and lots more. Check site for more details…

Bonner Scholars Program: Bonner Scholars receive substantial grant and scholarship assistance to meet their *financial need in full*.

Requirements: Top Applicants

Check site for more details…

Army ROTC Scholarship: Awards full tuition and fees. In addition to the awarded scholarship, each winner receives a flat rate of $1,200 annually for books and supplies, as well as a tax-free monthly stipend.

Requirements: Top applicants | Applicant must be a U.S citizen.

Application Deadline: November 15

Application link: https://www.wofford.edu/admission/scholarships

SOUTH CAROLINA

9 Clemson University

Location: Clemson, South Carolina
Setting: Suburban (17,000 Acres)
Undergraduate Enrollment: 20,840
Type: Public

National Scholars Program: Full tuition, fees, room & board, and other expenses.

Criteria: Selection is based on a review of top applications to the Clemson University Honors College and a rigorous interview process.

Application Deadline: December 15

Application link: https://www.clemson.edu/financial-aid/types/scholarships/clemson-scholarship-recruiting.html

10 Francis Marion University

Location: Florence, South Carolina
Setting: Rural (832 Acres)
Undergraduate Enrollment: 3,632
Type: Public

Robert E. McNair Scholarship: Awards Full tuition, housing, and a meal plan. It also offers funding for a study abroad experience.

Requirements: Top scholars in applicants' pool.

Application Deadline: December 1

Application link: https://www.fmarion.edu/financialassistance/scholarships/

11 University of South Carolina

Location: Columbia, South Carolina
Setting: City (444 Acres)
Undergraduate Enrollment: 27,270
Type: Public

Gamecock Guarantee: Award covers full cost of tuition and technology fees.

Eligibility: Applicant must be a South Carolina resident and come from a **low-income** family.

Application Deadline: December 1

Application link: https://sc.edu/about/offices_and_divisions/undergraduate_admissions/tuition_scholarships/scholarships/guarantee/index.php

SOUTH CAROLINA

12 Claflin University

Location: Orangeburg, South Carolina
Setting: City (46 Acres)
Undergraduate Enrollment: 1,969
Type: Private

Claflin Presidential Scholars Program: Awards Full tuition, room, board, textbooks and a monthly stipend.

Requirements: A minimum SAT score of 1200 or ACT equivalent score of 27.

Claflin Honors College Scholarship: Award value ranges from $2,000 to the full cost of tuition, room and board.

Requirements: A minimum SAT score of 1100 or ACT equivalent score of 24.

Application Deadline: July 31

Application link: https://www.claflin.edu/admissions-aid/financial-aid/scholarships-and-grants

13 College of Charleston

Location: Charleston, South Carolina
Setting: Urban (80 Acres)
Undergraduate Enrollment: 9,300
Type: Public

There are lot's of scholarship opportunities available for undergraduate study at the College of Charleston, please refer to this site for more information: https://admissions.cofc.edu/applyingtothecollege/international-students/tuition.php

P.S: The value for most of the scholarships weren't attached.

14 Erskine College

Location: Due West, South Carolina
Setting: Rural (90 Acres)
Undergraduate Enrollment: 809
Type: Private

Presidential Scholarship: Awards Full tuition, required fees, room and board.

Requirements: Top applicants.

Application Deadline: October 15

Application link: https://www.erskine.edu/admissions-aid/financial-aid/sc-scholarships/

SOUTH DAKOTA

University of South Dakota

Location: Vermillion, South Dakota
Setting: Rural (274 Acres)
Undergraduate Enrollment: 7,103
Type: Public

Academic Achievement Scholarships:

Mickelson Scholarships: Award covers full tuition, general fees, double occupancy room and board.

Requirements: Scholarship recipients must be residents of South Dakota | A minimum ACT score of 28 (1320 SAT)

George S. Mickelson Scholarship: Awards Full tuition, general fees, double occupancy room (funded by a Housing Scholarship) and standard board charges for four years.

Requirements: Scholarship recipients must be residents of South Dakota | A minimum ACT score of 28 (1320 SAT)

Field of Study Scholarships:

Dorothy C. Schieffer Political Science Scholarship: Awards full tuition, fees, books, room and board. At least one international travel or study abroad experience and a working internship or service opportunity may be included after consultation with faculty advisor and non-faculty mentor.

Criteria: Awarded to full-time students who major or minor in political science.

Nolop Institute Scholarship for Medical Biology: Awards in-state tuition, fees, room, board and books for up to four years of full-time study.

Eligibility: This scholarship is awarded to a talented and ambitious student majoring in medical biology who wishes to participate in meaningful research with plans to attend medical school.

Reserve Officers Training Corp (ROTC): Awards full tuition, money for books and a non-taxed monthly stipend.

Application Deadline: November 15

Application link:
https://www.usd.edu/Admissions-and-Aid/Financial-Aid/Types-of-Aid/Scholarships/

TENNESEEE

1. Vanderbilt University

Location: Nashville, Tennessee
Setting: Urban (333 Acres)
Undergraduate Enrollment: 7,057
Type: Private

Chancellor's Scholars: Full tuition, plus a one-time summer stipend for an immersive experience following the sophomore or junior year.

Cornelius Vanderbilt Scholarship: Full tuition, plus a one-time summer stipend for an immersive experience following the sophomore or junior year.

Ingram Scholars Program: Full tuition, plus a stipend for a special summer service project.

Requirements for the Above Scholarships: Top students from applicants pool.

Application Deadline: December 1

Application link: https://www.vanderbilt.edu/scholarships/

2. Union University

Location: Jackson, Tennessee
Setting: City (360 Acres)
Undergraduate Enrollment: 2,096
Type: Private

Founders Scholarship: Awards full tuition, room & board, meals and student services fees for credit hours taken during Fall and Spring terms for a maximum of eight undergraduate semesters.

Scholars of Excellence Awards: All applicants who meet the requirements for Scholars of Excellence and participate in the on-campus competition weekend will be awarded a Scholars of Excellence Award that may be combined with all other institutional aid.

P.S: No student will be awarded beyond the cost of attendance through a combination of institutional and non-institutional source.

Requirements: 29 ACT minimum score or a minimum SAT score of 1330 | 3.5 minimum high school GPA.

ROTC Programs

Army ROTC scholarship: Awards full tuition, $1,200 annually for books, supplies and equipment, as well as $420/month tax-free stipend.

Requirements: U.S. citizen | GPA of 2.5 or better.

Application Deadline: January 5

Application link: https://www.uu.edu/financialaid/scholarships/

TENNESEEE

3. Belmont University

Location: Nashville, Tennessee
Setting: Urban (93 Acres)
Undergraduate Enrollment: 6,626
Type: Private

Archer Presidential Scholarship: Awards Full tuition, fees, books, room & board for four academic years.

Requirements: Top Applicants.

William Randolph Hearst Endowed Scholarship: Awards Full tuition, fees, books, room & board.

Eligibility: A freshman student from a diverse background.

Requirements: Top Applicants.

Application Deadline: December 1

Application link: https://www.belmont.edu/sfs/scholarships/merit.html

4. Middle Tennessee State University

Location: Murfreesboro, Tennessee
Setting: City (550 Acres)
Undergraduate Enrollment: 19,188
Type: Public

The ROTC Opportunity: Awards Full tuition, fees, $1200 per year for books, monthly stipend for every month school is in session up to $5,000 per year, Eligibility for room and board scholarship for up to $4,000 dollars a year.

Eligibility: Applicant must be a U.S. citizen | Be between the ages of 17 and 26.

Requirements: A minimum high school GPA of 2.50 | Have a high school diploma or equivalent | Meet physical standards and be medically qualified.

Application Deadline: October 1

Application link: https://www.mtsu.edu/arotc1/scholarships/index.php

TENNESEEE

5. University of Sewanee

Location: Sewanee, Tennessee
Setting: Rural (13,000 Acres)
Undergraduate Enrollment: 1,716
Type: Private

Vice-Chancellor's Scholarship: Awards Full tuition, fees, room and board annually.

Benedict Scholarship: Awards Full tuition, fees, room and board annually.

Requirements: Top scholars from applicants pool.

Application Deadline: January 15

Application link:
https://new.sewanee.edu/admission-aid/cost-financial-aid/scholarships/

6. Bryan College

Location: Dayton, Tennessee
Setting: Rural (128 Acres)
Undergraduate Enrollment: 1,241
Type: Private

Bryan Opportunity Scholarship Program: Award covers Full tuition, room & board.

Requirements: A minimum cumulative high school GPA of 3.75 and ACT 29 or SAT 1330

Application Deadline: December 15

Application link:
https://www.bryan.edu/scholarship/bryan-opportunity-scholarship-program/

TEXAS

1. University of Texas at Tyler

Location: Tyler, Texas
Setting: City (320 Acres)
Undergraduate Enrollment: 7,237
Type: Public

Presidential Fellow: Full tuition, fees, books, room and board.

Criteria: 3.75+ high school GPA

Application Deadline: December 1

Valedictorian Scholarship: Full tuition, fees, books, room & board.

Criteria: Applicant must be Valedictorian from high school residing in Smith County, or the cities of Palestine or Longview.

Salutatorian Scholarship: Full tuition & fees.

Criteria: Applicant must be Salutatorian from high school residing in Smith County, or the cities of Palestine or Longview.

Need Based Scholarship: Full tuition and Mandatory fees.

Criteria: Applicant must be a dependent member of a household whose parent's adjusted gross income is $80,000 or lower.

Application Deadline: June 1

Application link:
https://www.uttyler.edu/scholarships/freshman/new-freshman-20-21.php

2. University of Texas at Austin

Location: Austin, Texas
Setting: Urban (437 Acres)
Undergraduate Enrollment: 40,048
Type: Public

Forty Acres Scholars Program: A full ride scholarship that covers the total cost of attendance.

Requirements: Applicant must be a U.S citizen or permanent U.S. resident at the time of application.

Application Deadline: November 1

Application link:
https://www.texasexes.org/scholarships

TEXAS

Baylor University

Location: Waco, Texas
Setting: City (1,000 Acres)
Undergraduate Enrollment: 14,399
Type: Private

Getterman Scholars Program: Awards Full tuition, fees, room & board, along with support for study abroad, research and mission/service experiences.

Requirements: Top students from applicants poo

Application Deadline: November 1

Application link: https://www.baylor.edu/honorscollege/index.php?id=959651

Texas State University

Location: San Marcos, Texas
Setting: Suburban (507 Acres)
Undergraduate Enrollment: 33,193
Type: Public

Terry Foundation Scholarship: Awards Full academic scholarship up to the total cost of attendance.

Requirements: Top applicants | Applicant must be a U.S. Citizen or permanent resident and demonstrate financial need | Will graduate from a Texas high school or home-school program in Texas.

Application Deadline: December 15

Application link: https://www.finaid.txst.edu/scholarships/freshman/comp.html

TEXAS

5 Southern Methodist University

Location: Dallas, Texas
Setting: Urban (234 Acres)
Undergraduate Enrollment: 6,827
Type: Private

President's Scholars Program: Awards full tuition and fees plus study abroad stipend. Students who live on campus also receive a scholarship for room and board.

Requirements: Top applicants

Application Deadline: November 1

Application link: https://www.smu.edu/EnrollmentServices/financialaid/TypesOfAid/Scholarships

6 Texas Woman's University

Location: Denton, Texas
Setting: City (270 Acres)
Undergraduate Enrollment: 10,656
Type: Public

Terry Foundation Scholarship: Full tuition, fees, room and board on campus, books, and supplies.

Requirements: Applicant must be a U.S. Citizen or permanent resident and demonstrate financial need | 3.0 minimum high school GPA | Will graduate from a Texas high school or home-school program in Texas.

Chancellor's Endowed Scholarship: Full tuition, mandatory fees, and a book stipend for up to four years.

Requirements: Top scholars from applicants pool.

TWU Presidential Scholarship: Full tuition and mandatory fees for up to four years.

Eligibility: Awarded to freshmen who are Valedictorian or Salutatorian of an accredited high school class.

Application Deadline: March 15

Application link: https://catalog.twu.edu/undergraduate/financial-aid/scholarships/

TEXAS

7. Texas Christian University

Location: Fort Worth, Texas
Setting: Suburban (302 Acres)
Undergraduate Enrollment: 9,474
Type: Private

Chancellor's Scholarship: Full tuition & fees.

Requirements: Top students from applicants pool.

NAACP Scholarship: Full tuition and fees for up to four years.

Eligibility: Applicant must be planning to pursue a degree in education and make a 3 year commitment to teach in the FWISD.

John V. Roach Family Endowement: Provides full room, board and books for top students in the class who have been offered full tuition from another academic scholarship.

Trustee Scholarship: Combines with other academic awards to provide a full scholarship covering room, board and books.

Please refer to this site for more details: https://tcu.smartcatalogiq.com/en/Current/Undergraduate-Catalog/Student-Financial-Aid/Academic-Scholarships

Application Deadline: Applicant's are highly encouraged to apply Early Action.

Application link: https://financialaid.tcu.edu/types-of-aid/scholarships/index.php

8. University of Houston

Location: Houston, Texas
Setting: Urban (895 Acres)
Undergraduate Enrollment: 39,165
Type: Public

Tier One Scholars: Award covers full tuition and mandatory fees, on-campus housing and meal plan for the first two years, $1,000 stipend to support undergraduate research, $2,000 stipend to support learning abroad and lot's more.

Requirements: Top applicants

National Merit Scholarship Finalist: Full tuition and required fees, plus a one-time $1,000 undergraduate research stipend and a one-time $2,000 study abroad stipend.

Eligibility: Awarded to National Merit Scholarship finalists who select the University of Houston as their first-choice institution.

Application Deadline: November 8

Application link: https://uh.edu/financial/undergraduate/types-aid/scholarships/

TEXAS

9 Prairie View A & M University

Location: Prairie View, Texas
Setting: Rural (1,502 Acres)
Undergraduate Enrollment: 8,109
Type: Public

Regent's Student Merit Scholarship: The Regent's scholarship covers up to $10,000 per academic year for tuition and mandatory fees. Each Regent Scholar will receive additional Scholarship funding to meet the cost for up to 18 credit hours, on campus housing, meals and books ($600 per semester).

Requirements: Applicant must have graduated from a high school within 12 months of enrolling at Prairie View A & M University | A minimum 3.50 cumulative high school GPA | A minimum SAT score of 1260 or ACT composite score of 26.

Application Deadline: December 1

Application link: https://www.pvamu.edu/oss/

10 University of Texas at Arlington

Location: Arlington, Texas
Setting: Urban (420 Acres)
Undergraduate Enrollment: 35,064
Type: Public

National Merit: Award covers Full tuition, fees, on-campus housing, and includes a stipend for books, supplies, and other educational expenses for fall and spring semesters.

Requirements: National Merit recipient.

Application Deadline: February 14

Application link: https://www.uta.edu/administration/fao/scholarships

TEXAS

University of Texas at Dallas

Location: Richardson, Texas
Setting: Suburban (500 Acres)
Undergraduate Enrollment: 21,187
Type: Public

Academic Excellence Scholarship Program: Full ride scholarship.

Eugene McDermott Scholars Program: Awards full scholarship plus a stipend package.

Terry Foundation Scholarship: A full ride scholarship that covers the total cost of undergraduate studies.

Requirements: Top applicants

Application Deadline: December 1

National Merit Scholars Program: Award covers full tuition and mandatory fees, $4,000 per semester cash stipend to defray the costs of books, supplies and other expenses, $1,500 per semester on-campus housing stipend, one-time study abroad stipend up to $6,000 to support an international education experience.

Requirements: Applicant must be named a National Merit Finalist by the National Merit scholarship Corporation | List UT Dallas as their first-choice school through the National Merit Scholarship Corporation online portal.

Application Deadline: July 31

Application link: https://finaid.utdallas.edu/scholarships/

University of Utah

Location: Salt Lake City, Utah
Setting: Urban (1,534 Acres)
Undergraduate Enrollment: 24,643
Type: Public

FOR UTAH Scholarship Program: Awards Full tuition and fees to Utah residents who are eligible for the Pell Grant.

Eligibility: Utah residents | High school average GPA of at least 3.2

Application Deadline: February 1
Application link: https://admissions.utah.edu/forutah/

University of Vermont

Location: Burlington, Vermont
Setting: Suburban (460 Acres)
Undergraduate Enrollment: 11,136
Type: Public

Army ROTC Scholarships: Award covers full tuition and fees.

Air Force ROTC Scholarships: Award covers full tuition and fees.

Eligibility: Applicant must be a U.S. citizen | Eligibility determined by ROTC.

Application Deadline: January 10

Application link:
https://www.uvm.edu/studentfinancialservices/prospective_undergraduate_student_scholarships_requiring_separate

VIRGINIA

1. College of William & Mary

Location: Williamsburg, Virginia
Setting: Suburban (1,200 Acres)
Undergraduate Enrollment: 6,377
Type: Public

1693 Scholars Program: Award covers the cost of in-state tuition, general fees, room and board plus a $5,000 stipend to support independent projects.

Requirements: Applicant must rank in the top 1% of their graduating high school class | 33+ ACT or 1500+ SAT (Test Optional).

William & Mary Scholars: Awards are worth the amount of in-state tuition and fees.

Application Deadline: April 1
Application link:
https://www.wm.edu/admission/undergraduateadmission/costs-aid/scholarship/index.php

2. University of Richmond

Location: Richmond, Virginia
Setting: Suburban (350 Acres)
Undergraduate Enrollment: 3,161
Type: Private

Richmond Scholars Program: Full tuition, room and board (in addition to other program benefits)

Requirements: Top applicants

Richmond's Promise to Virginia: Awards full tuition, room, and the Spider Unlimited meal plan for **Virginia resident's.**

Eligibility: U.S. citizens or U.S. permanent residents | Qualify for need-based financial aid.

Application Deadline: December 1
Application link:
https://financialaid.richmond.edu/

VIRGINIA

3. Virginia State University

Location: Petersburg, Virginia
Setting: Suburban (231 Acres)
Undergraduate Enrollment: 4,025
Type: Public

The Four-Year Army ROTC Scholarship Program: Award covers full tuition and fees or Housing and Living Allowance, a $1,200 yearly book allowance, ROTC stipends of $420 a month.

Criteria: Applicant must be 17 years before scholarship is effective | A minimum 1,000 SAT score or ACT composite score of 19 | A minimum high school GPA of 2.5 or higher.

Requirements: Top applicants.

Application Deadline: December 15

Application link: https://www.vsu.edu/sola/departments/military-science/benefits.php

4. Washington & Lee University

Location: Lexington City, Virginia
Setting: City (430 Acres)
Undergraduate Enrollment: 1,829
Type: Private

The Johnson Scholarship: Award covers Full tuition, room & board. Johnson Scholars receive funding up to $7,000 to support summer experiences during their time at W&L.

P.S: Students with financial need higher than this amount will have any additional need met by the scholarship.

Requirements: Top applicants.

Regional Scholarships

Darnall W. Boyd Jr. Memorial Honor Scholarship: Awards Full tuition, room and board.

P.S: This scholarship was established for entering first-year students from *South Carolina*, with a preference for students from the *Columbia area*.

Requirements: Top applicants.

Application Deadline: December 1

Application link: https://www.wlu.edu/admissions/scholarships-and-aid/

VIRGINIA

5 Virginia Technology University

Location: Blacksburg, Virginia
Setting: Rural (2,600 Acres)
Undergraduate Enrollment: 30,020
Type: Public

Presidential Scholarship Program: Award covers Full tuition, fees, room and board, a structured, well established academic support and enrichment, plus a lot of other benefits.

Eligibility: Applicant must be a **Virginia resident** | Graduate from a **Virginia high school** | Be Pell grant eligible with significant financial need | Demonstrate potential for stellar academic performance | Show evidence of leadership potential.

Requirements: Top Students.

Application link: https://finaid.vt.edu/undergraduate/typesofaid/scholarships/presidential-scholarship-programs.html

Stamps Scholars: Award covers Full tuition, fees, room and board.

Eligibility: Stamps Scholars.

Application link: https://honorscollege.vt.edu/Scholarships/recruitment/Stamps.html

Military Scholarships

Army ROTC: Award covers Full tuition, mandatory fees, $1,200 per year for textbooks, supplies and equipment; and a monthly stipend of $420 per month depending on the student's academic year.

Eligibility: Applicant must be a U.S. citizen, and both medically and physically qualified to be eligible.

Air Force (AFROTC) and Naval ROTC scholarships are also available.

Application Deadline: January 15

Application link: https://finaid.vt.edu/undergraduate/typesofaid/scholarships/military-scholarships.html

VIRGINIA

6 Hampden-Sydney College

Location: Hampden Sydney, Virginia
Setting: Rural (1,343 Acres)
Undergraduate Enrollment: 881
Type: Private

Madison Scholarship: Award covers Full tuition, fees, room (double occupancy) & board for four years. Plus a stipend for books and a tablet, and funding for either a summer internship, or a study abroad opportunity.

Requirements: A minimum high school GPA of 4.0 | Reading and Mathematics SAT score of 1450+, or an ACT composite score of 32+ | Class rank in the top 5% (if reported)

Application Deadline: January 15

Application link: https://www.hsc.edu/admission-and-financial-aid/financial-aid/types-of-aid/academic-and-leadership-awards/

7 Virginia Military Institute

Location: Lexington City, Virginia
Setting: City (200 Acres)
Undergraduate Enrollment: 1,698
Type: Military

Peay Merit Scholarships: Awards full tuition, fees, room and board.

Requirements: A minimum High school GPA of 3.75

Application Deadline: February 1

Application link: https://www.vmi.edu/academics/institute-scholars/

8 Virginia Commonwealth University

Location: Richmond, Virginia
Setting: Urban (168 Acres)
Undergraduate Enrollment: 21,943
Type: Public

Presidential Scholarship: Award covers Full tuition, fees, room and board.

Requirements: A average GPA of 4.59 | Average SAT score of 1513.

Application Deadline: November 1

Application link: https://admissions.vcu.edu/cost-aid/scholarships-funding/

VIRGINIA

9. University of Virginia

Location: Charlottesville, Virginia
Setting: Suburban (1,682 Acres)
Undergraduate Enrollment: 17,311
Type: Public

Jefferson Scholarship: Awards full tuition, room and board plus a funding for research, summer experiences, study abroad, etc. There are also extensive enrichment and programming opportunities for Jefferson Scholars.

Criteria: The Jefferson Scholarship is awarded through the Jefferson Scholars Foundation | Top applicants.

UVA Questbridge Scholarship: A full ride scholarship.

Requirements: Applicant must demonstrate financial need and have satisfactory academic performance

Application Deadline: November 1

Application link: https://www.jeffersonscholars.org/

10. Hampton University

Location: Hampton, Virginia
Setting: Urban (314 Acres)
Undergraduate Enrollment: 3,063
Type: Private

Reserve Officer's Training Corps (ROTC):

Army ROTC Scholarship: Awards full tuition and mandatory fees plus a monthly stipend. Also Cadets receive $1,200 annually for textbooks.

Navy ROTC Scholarship: Awards full tuition and mandatory fees. Also Navy cadets will receive a $400 monthly stipend as well as funding for textbooks.

Hampton University awards merit based scholarships that range from $5,000 - $25,000 per academic year. These generous award amounts are designed to provide many awards to a vast number of students, as opposed to awarding a few large amounts to a smaller population. Hence, the University no longer has scholarships that are named Trustee, Presidential, Legacy, etc.

Application Deadline: November 1

Application link: https://home.hamptonu.edu/admissions/

WASHINGTON

1 American University

Location: Washington, D.C
Setting: Suburban (84 Acres)
Undergraduate Enrollment: 7,953
Type: Private

American University District Scholars Award: Covers full tuition, room and board.

Requirements: Applicant must be a DC resident attending a DC Public or Public Charter High School | Top Applicants.

Frederick Douglass Distinguished Scholars Program: Full tuition, room and board, meal plan, books, mandatory fees and public transportation (U-Pass)

Requirements: A minimum 3.8 GPA (unweighted) or 4.0 GPA (weighted)

P.S: Submission of ACT or SAT scores are optional.

Application Deadline: December 15

Application link: https://www.american.edu/financialaid/freshman-scholarships.cfm

2 Howard University

Location: Washington, D.C
Setting: Urban (257 Acres)
Undergraduate Enrollment: 6,526
Type: Public

Howard University Freshman Scholarship: HU Presidential Scholarship | HU Founders Scholarship | HU Capstone Scholarship | HU Leadership Scholarship | HU Opportunity Grant

These scholarships can cover the cost of up to full tuition, fees, room, board and book voucher, etc.

Requirements: Top scholars in applicants' pool.

Please refer to this site for more details: https://www2.howard.edu/student-financial-services/scholarships-and-grants

Application Deadline: March 27

Application link: https://www2.howard.edu/student-financial-services/funding-opportunities

WASHINGTON

3. George Washington University

Location: Washington, D.C
Setting: Urban (43 Acres)
Undergraduate Enrollment: 11,762
Type: Private

District Scholars: This Scholarship makes it possible for the University to meet full demonstrated need for qualifying residents of the District of Columbia.

Eligibility: Applicant must be a resident of the District and qualify for the D.C. Tuition Assistance Grant | Have an annual family income as determined by George Washington that does not exceed $75,000.

Stephen Joel Trachtenberg Scholarship: Awards Full tuition, room and board, books and fees.

Eligibility: Applicant must be a *District of Columbia* resident | Attend a regionally accredited secondary school in the District of Columbia.

P.S: Students must apply to GW by January 5 and be nominated by their high school counselor by January 11

Scholars are selected based on academic record, including GPA, course of study, teacher recommendations, leadership qualities, community service, and other extracurricular activities and achievements.

Application Deadline: January 5
Application link: https://undergraduate.admissions.gwu.edu/merit-scholarships

4. Pacific Lutheran University

Location: Tacoma, Washington
Setting: Suburban (156 Acres)
Undergraduate Enrollment: 2,544
Type: Private

Army ROTC Scholarship: Awards full tuition, on campus room/meals.

Requirements: Top scholars.

P.S: Applicants must file FAFSA for on-campus living costs to be covered.

Application Deadline: October 15
Application link: https://www.plu.edu/student-financial-services/types-of-aid/scholarships-and-grants/

WASHINGTON

5. University of Puget Sound

Location: Tacoma, Washington
Setting: Urban (97 Acres)
Undergraduate Enrollment: 1,898
Type: Private

Matelich Scholarship: Awards Full tuition and fees, (standard double room, standard medium meal plan, and student government fee) for up to four years.

Requirements: Top scholars in applicants' pool.

Application Deadline: December 1

Application link: https://www.pugetsound.edu/admission/cost-aid/types-aid/scholarships-grants/matelich-scholarship-puget-sound

6. The Catholic University of America

Location: Washington, D.C
Setting: Urban (176 Acres)
Undergraduate Enrollment: 3,055
Type: Private

ROTC Scholarships: Students who earn Full tuition *ROTC Scholarships* from the Army, Navy, or Air Force will automatically be eligible for the ROTC Room and Board Matching Scholarship.

Requirements: Top Applicants

Application Deadline: March 30

Application link: https://www.catholic.edu/admission/undergraduate/first-year-students/scholarships/index.html

WASHINGTON

7. Seattle University

Location: Seattle, Washington
Setting: Urban (50 Acres)
Undergraduate Enrollment: 4,299
Type: Private

Sullivan Leadership Award: Awards Full tuition, room and board for four years.

Requirements: A minimum high school GPA of 3.7 | U.S. residents.

P.S: Consideration is reserved for first-year students living in and attending school in the United States.

Fostering Scholars: Award covers Full tuition, books, and other education related expenses, Waiver of all enrollment related fees, Student health insurance (if needed), Assistance finding on-campus employment opportunities, Assistance finding on-campus employment opportunities, plus other benefits.

Eligibility: Applicant must be a **Washington State** resident.

Requirements: Top applicants.

Application Deadline: March 1

Application link: https://www.seattleu.edu/undergraduate-admissions/finances/scholarships/freshmen/

8. Gonzaga University

Location: Spokane, Washington
Setting: City (152 Acres)
Undergraduate Enrollment: 4,852
Type: Private

Army ROTC Scholarship: Awards Fully paid Dorm room, Fully paid Boarding (Meal Plan), $600 a semester for books, a $420 per month Monthly stipend (non-taxed), a $40 waiver of the university application fee, plus other benefits.

Requirements: Top students in applicants pool.

Application Deadline: December 15

Application link: https://www.gonzaga.edu/academics/undergraduate/military-science/scholarships

WEST VIRGINIA

1. West Liberty University

Location: West Liberty, West Virginia
Setting: Rural (290 Acres)
Undergraduate Enrollment: 2,125
Type: Public

Full Ride Elbin Scholarship: Full tuition, mandatory fees, base room and board.

Requirements: Minimum high school GPA of 4.0 | 30 ACT or 1400 SAT.

Bessie Anderson College of Education Honors Scholarship: Covers the cost of tuition, fees, room and board.

Eligibility: West Virginia resident | Minimum high school GPA of 3.5.

Application Deadline: April 15

Application link: https://westliberty.edu/financial-aid/west-liberty-university-scholarships/

2. Fairmont State University

Location: Fairmont, West Virginia
Setting: City (120 Acres)
Undergraduate Enrollment: 3,573
Type: Public

Charles J. McClain Presidential Scholarship: Awards Full tuition, fees, room and board for on-campus students, and a $500/per semester book scholarship for the on-campus Bound for Success Bookstore.

Eligibility: Applicant must be a **West Virginia** Student | Be a PROMISE Scholarship recipient.

Requirements: A minimum cumulative high school GPA of 3.5 | Have ACT composite score of 26+ or 1190+ SAT (combined Critical Reading and Math scores) or 1260+ SAT total score.

Application Deadline: February 1

Application link: https://www.fairmontstate.edu/finaid/funding/charles-j-mcclain-presidential-scholarship

WEST VIRGINIA

3. University of Charleston

Location: Charleston, West Virginia
Setting: City
Undergraduate Enrollment: 2,115
Type: Private

Presidential Scholarship: Awards Full tuition, mandatory fees, room and board for four years. In addition to incredible financial support, the Presidential Scholarship also provides you with the opportunity to meet regularly with UC President Roth for mentoring and leadership skill development.

Requirements: A minimum high school GPA of 3.75 | A demonstrated record of leadership and citizenship | A desire to become a campus leader while serving the UC & Charleston communities.

Application Deadline: December 15

Application link:
https://www.ucwv.edu/presidential-scholarship/

4. West Virginia State University

Location: Institute, West Virginia
Setting: Suburban (100 Acres)
Undergraduate Enrollment: 4,009
Type: Public

Presidential Scholarship: Awards Full tuition, fees, room and board for four years.

Eligibility: Enrollment in an academic degree program in a Science, Technology, Engineering or Mathematics (STEM) or Healthcare Field.

Requirements: A minimum high school GPA of 3.5 (4.0 scale)

Application Deadline: March 31

Application link:
https://www.wvstateu.edu/admissions/scholarships.aspx

WISCONSIN

1. University of Wisconsin

Location: Madison, Wisconsin
Setting: City (936 Acres)
Undergraduate Enrollment: 33,456
Type: Public

International Scholarships

King-Morgridge Scholars Program: Awards full tuition and fees, on-campus room and board, health insurance, airfare, and a stipend for miscellaneous expenses.

Eligibility: King-Morgridge Scholars will hail from countries in Africa, the Caribbean, Latin America, South and Southeast Asia.

There are lot's of scholarship opportunities available for undergraduate study at the University of Wisconsin.

Please refer to this site for more details: https://financialaid.wisc.edu/types-of-aid/scholarships/

Application Deadline: February 8
Application link: https://admissions.wisc.edu/international-scholarships/

2. Carthage College

Location: Kenosha, Wisconsin
Setting: Suburban (80 Acres)
Undergraduate Enrollment: 2,641
Type: Private

There are competitive scholarships available for undergraduate studies at the Carthage College.

Applicant's can win scholarships ranging from 75 percent of tuition to full tuition, room, and board through a variety of scholarship competitions.

Requirements: Top applicants.

Application Deadline: December 3
Application link: https://www.carthage.edu/admissions/undergraduate-students/undergraduate-scholarships/presidential-scholarship-program/

WISCONSIN

3. Edgewood College

Location: Madison, Wisconsin
Setting: City (55 Acres)
Undergraduate Enrollment: 1,407
Type: Private

Community Scholars Award: Awards Full tuition + 1st & 2nd Year room and board.

Eligibility: Underrepresented, BIPOC, or 1st generation students graduating from a Dane County high school are encouraged to apply.

P.S: You must be a resident of Dane County to apply.

Requirements: Top applicants.

Application Deadline: December 1

Application link:
https://www.edgewood.edu/admissions/tuition-and-financial-aid/freshman-scholarships

4. St. Norbert College

Location: De Pere, Wisconsin
Setting: Suburban (116 Acres)
Undergraduate Enrollment: 1,867
Type: Private

Army ROTC Scholarship: Awards Full tuition, room and board plus additional allowances for books and fees.

Requirements: Top applicants.

Application Deadline: January 20

Application link:
https://www.snc.edu/militaryscience/awards.html

WISCONSIN

5 University of Wisconsin, Milwaukee

Location: Milwaukee, Wisconsin
Setting: Urban (261 Acres)
Undergraduate Enrollment: 20,213
Type: Public

Anu and Satya Nadella Scholarship: Award covers Full tuition, fees, room and board for up to five years.

Eligibility: Applicant must be a graduate from a public or private high school in the city of Milwaukee | Admitted to UWM as a freshman in one of the following majors: BS Applied Mathematics and Computer Science, BS Computer Engineering, BA or BS Computer Science, BS Data science, BS Information Science & Technology, BBA Information Technology Management.

Demonstrated Academic merit or potential

Demonstrated Financial need.

Requirements: Top applicants.

Application Deadline: August 15

Application link: https://uwm.edu/undergrad-admission/scholarships-aid/

6 Mount Mary University

Location: Milwaukee, Wisconsin
Setting: Urban (80 Acres)
Undergraduate Enrollment: 636
Type: Private

Caroline Scholars Program: Awards Full tuition, room and board for four years.

Requirements: A minimum cumulative, unweighted High school GPA of 3.5

Check site for more details…

Application Deadline: January 1

Application link: https://mtmary.edu/costs-aid/scholarships/index.html

WISCONSIN

7 University of Wisconsin, Platteville

Location: Platteville, Wisconsin
Setting: Rural (820 Acres)
Undergraduate Enrollment: 7,479
Type: Public

Capstan Scholarship: Awards Full tuition, room and board.

Requirements: A cumulative GPA of 2.0-3.25.

Eligibility: Applicant must be a U.S. Citizen | Applicant must be pursuing a bachelor's degree in a STEM field, Accounting, or Finance | Applicant's hometown must be in the heart of the Midwestern United States, this includes the following states: Wisconsin, Iowa, Illinois, Minnesota, or Michigan | Applicant must show need based on the FAFSA.

Check site for more details…

Application Deadline: April 1
Application link: https://www.uwplatt.edu/types-scholarships#freshman-scholarships

8 Milwaukee School of Engineering

Location: Milwaukee, Wisconsin
Setting: Urban (22 Acres)
Undergraduate Enrollment: 2,510
Type: Private

MSOE Presidential Scholarship: Awards Full tuition, room and board for four years.

Requirements: A minimum unweighted High school GPA of 3.5 on a (4.0 scale)

P.S: Currently, International Students are *not* eligible to receive the Presidential scholarship.

Application Deadline: October 25
Application link: https://www.msoe.edu/admissions-aid/financial-aid-scholarships/scholarships-and-grants/msoe-scholarships-grants/

Marquette University

Location: Milwaukee, Wisconsin
Setting: Urban (107 Acres)
Undergraduate Enrollment: 8,024
Type: Private

Ann Kenny Carr Cristo Rey Scholarship: Awards Full tuition, room and board for four years.

Eligibility: Awarded to graduates of Cristo Rey Pilsen High School.

Requirements: Top students in applicant pool.

Do Great Things Full Tuition Scholarship: Awards Full tuition and 2 years of room (on-campus, standard double occupancy) and board.

Eligibility: Applicant must attend Green Bay West High School | Demonstrated financial need as determined by the Free Application for Federal Student Aid or Net Price Calculator.

Requirements: Top Applicants

The Donald J. and Frances I. Herdrich Endowed Scholarship for Engineering: Awards Full tuition, fees, on-campus housing and meals to students with financial need who are admitted to the *Opus College of Engineering.*

Requirements: Top applicants

P.S: Priority will be given to first-generation students (i.e. neither parent graduated from college)

Application Deadline: December 1
Application link: https://www.marquette.edu/explore/scholarships.php

University of Wyoming

Location: Laramie, Wyoming
Setting: Suburban (2,021 Acres)
Undergraduate Enrollment: 9,342
Type: Public

Trustees Scholars Award: Awards full tuition, mandatory fees, university room and board.

Eligibility: Wyoming Residents | Applicants must demonstrate or have a track record of excellence.

Application Deadline: January 5

Application link: https://www.uwyo.edu/sfa/scholarships/residents/trustees.html

CHAPTER 2

FULL RIDE EXTERNAL $CHOLARSHIP$

Morehead-Cain Scholarship

OVERVIEW

Morehead-Cain Scholarship Program — A fully-funded educational experience without peers. This scholarship is awarded annually, covering the student's *tuition, room and board* expenses for four years of undergraduate study. It offers (and funds) life-changing summer enrichment and extracurricular learning experiences. It provides immersion in a dynamic student body at a world-class university. And, it promises a lifetime connection to an extraordinary community of Morehead-Cain's scattered throughout the world.

It is the first merit scholarship program established in the United States. Founded at the first public university in the United States. It provides a four-year, fully funded educational experience for exceptional student leaders at the University of North Carolina at Chapel Hill.

International students are eligible to apply for this scholarship. It is open to both in-state, out-of-state, and international applicants.

SPECIAL NOTE: Morehead-Cain is an equal opportunity organization. It is the policy of the Morehead-Cain Foundation not to discriminate against any nominee or applicant based on race, color, national origin, ancestry, gender, sexual orientation, age, religion, creed, disability, marital status, veteran status, political affiliation, or any other factor protected by law.

The deadline for this scholarship is October 1st.

FULL RIDE EXTERNAL SCHOLARSHIPS

Frequently Asked Questions

When does the Morehead-Cain Scholarship Application Open?

The Morehead-Cain Scholarship application opens by August. The deadline is usually by October 1.

What does the Morehead-Cain Scholarship Cover?

The Morehead-Cain is so much more than **tuition, room and board**. It unleashes your potential. It offers (and funds) life-changing summer enrichment and extracurricular learning experiences. It provides a four-year, fully funded educational experience for exceptional student leaders at the University of North Carolina at Chapel Hill.

I'm an international student, am I eligible to apply for the Morehead-Cain Scholarship?

Yes, international students are eligible to apply for this scholarship. It is open to both in-state, out-of-state, and international applicants.

How old is the Morehead-Cain?

The Morehead Foundation created the Morehead Scholarship Program in 1951. This was the first non-athletic merit scholarship program in the United States.

Selection Criteria

Primary Criterion: Academic Excellence

Secondary Criteria:

- Applicants should posses good LEADERSHIP qualities.
- CHARACTER – Courage, humility, Intergrity, maturity, perseverance, self-awareness, generosity, and Empathy – These are the core values of the Morehead-Cain Community.
- PHYSICAL VIGOR – You value what is gained – collaboration, sportsmanship, discipline, stamina, and persistence – by preparing for and engaging in competitions and performances.

P.S: Due consideration is given to nominees with physical limitations.

To apply for the Morehead-Cain Scholarship Program, you must be:

✓ On track to graduate High School in the Spring

✓ A competitive applicant to the University of North Carolina at Chapel Hill.

✓ Nominated by your High School or an Affiliate program, or applying directly.

View more Details and more information on the Morehead-Cain Scholarship Site.

☑ **Application Link: https://moreheadcain.org/**

2 Richmond Scholars Program

OVERVIEW

Richmond Scholars Program – The most prestigious academic merit award, given by the University of Richmond. This scholarship awards full tuition, room and board plus other program benefits. Scholars are defined by academic achievement, engaged leadership, strong sense of purpose, and investment in a diverse and inclusive campus community.

All applicants for first-year admission are automatically considered for this scholarship, provided that they submit a complete admission application by December 1st.

The final test dates accepted for Richmond Scholars' consideration are the October ACT and November SAT administrations.

The Richmond Scholars awards are funded by the University with the support of several endowments, including the Brockenbrough Family Scholarship, Elizabeth Ramos Dunkum Scholarship, Richard A. Mateer Scholarship, Oldham Scholars, Mildred Crowder Pickels Scholars Program, E. Claiborne Robins, Sr. Science Honors Scholarship, Guy A. Ross Scholarship, Minnie Roth Weinstein Memorial Scholars Program, and D. Chris Withers Merit Scholarship.

The goals of the Richmond Scholars program are to bring engaged, high-achieving students to campus and to retain those students through strong mentorship and programming.

The deadline for this scholarship is December 1st.

FULL RIDE EXTERNAL SCHOLARSHIPS

Frequently Asked Questions

When does the Richmond Scholars Program Application Open?

The final test dates accepted for Richmond Scholars consideration are the October ACT and November SAT administrations. The deadline is usually by December 1.

What does the Richmond Scholars Program Cover?

Richmond Scholars receive the University's most prestigious academic merit award, equal to full tuition, room and board plus other program benefits.

Program Benefits

- ✓ Full tuition, room and board, renewable for up to eight consecutive semesters of full-time enrollment
- ✓ Eligibility for a one-time $3,000 grant to support a student-selected activity that enhances the academic experience
- ✓ Priority course registration and guaranteed on-campus housing, and other benefits…

I am a current high school senior, am I eligible to apply?

An eligible student must be a candidate for high school graduation at the end of the current academic year, and plan to enroll in the University of Richmond.

Selection Criteria

Richmond Scholars will demonstrate a commitment to four main criteria, broadly defined:
- ➢ Academic Achievement
- ➢ Engaged Leadership
- ➢ Strong Sense of Purpose
- ➢ Interest in Diverse and Inclusive Community.

How old is the Richmond Scholars Program?

The University of Richmond has been awarding full-tuition, merit-based scholarships for decades. In 2000, the University created a new merit-based scholarships that would expand full-tuition scholarships. Some of these scholarships were endowed, others were funded through annual support.

I'm an international student, am I eligible to apply for the Richmond Scholars Program?

All applicants for first-year admission are automatically considered for this scholarship.

View more Details and more information on the Richmond Scholars Scholarship Site.

☑ **Application Link: https://scholars.richmond.edu/**

Jefferson Scholars Foundation

OVERVIEW

The mission of the Jefferson Scholars Foundation is to benefit the University of Virginia by identifying, attracting, and nurturing individuals of extraordinary intellectual range and depth who possess the highest qualities of leadership, scholarship, and citizenship.

The award for the Jefferson Scholarship is intended to cover the entire cost of attendance for four years at the University of Virginia, plus coverage of supplemental enrichment experiences.

The total value of the Jefferson Scholarship exceeds $333,000 for non-Virginian students and $177,000 for Virginian students. The stipends will exceed $72,000 for non-Virginian students and $36,000 for Virginian students.

The stipend includes tuition, fees, books, supplies, room, board, and personal expenses.

Jefferson Scholarship is awarded to individuals who have undergone a rigorous selection process and who possess an exceptional record of accomplishment both inside and outside the classroom.

P.S: No one may apply for the Jefferson Scholarship directly. Candidates must be nominated by their high schools (*Eligible High Schools*) based on their demonstrated excellence and exceptional potential in the areas of leadership, scholarship, and citizenship.

All counselors and Jefferson scholar nominees must submit a completed nomination form by December 1. Schools in the At-Large region have a separate deadline of November 15.

FULL RIDE EXTERNAL SCHOLARSHIPS

Frequently Asked Questions

When does the Jefferson Scholarship Application Open?

All counselors and Jefferson scholar nominees must submit a completed nomination form by December 1. Schools in the At-Large region have a separate deadline of November 15.

What does the Jefferson Scholarship Cover?

The award for the Jefferson Scholarship covers the **entire cost of attendance** for four years at the University of Virginia, plus coverage of supplemental enrichment experiences.

I'm an international student, am I eligible to apply for the Jefferson Scholarship?

Yes, International students are eligible for this scholarship. It is open to both in-state, out-of-state and international applicants. No one may apply for the Jefferson Scholarship directly. Candidates must be nominated by their high schools (*Eligible High Schools*) based on their demonstrated excellence and exceptional potential in the areas of leadership, scholarship, and citizenship.

P.S: Applicants are advised to check for the eligibility of their high school(s).

Selection Criteria

Jefferson Scholarship is awarded to individuals who have undergone a rigorous selection process and who possess an exceptional record of accomplishment both inside and outside the classroom.

No one may apply for the Jefferson Scholarship directly. Candidates must be nominated by their high schools (*Eligible High Schools*) based on their demonstrated excellence and exceptional potential in the areas of leadership, scholarship, and citizenship.

Once nominated, students are placed into regional competitions and may be invited to participate in one or more rounds of interviews. These interviews will determine the regional finalist(s) who will be invited to participate in the final stage of the Jefferson Scholarship competition.

How old is the Jefferson Scholarship?

The first Jefferson Scholarship was endowed in 1981, named after the benefactor of the University of Virginia, Thomas Jefferson. The program has grown since with the support of benefactors and endowments.

View more Details and more information on the Jefferson Scholars Foundation Scholarship Site.

☑ **Application Link: https://www.jeffersonscholars.org/**

Stamps Scholars Program

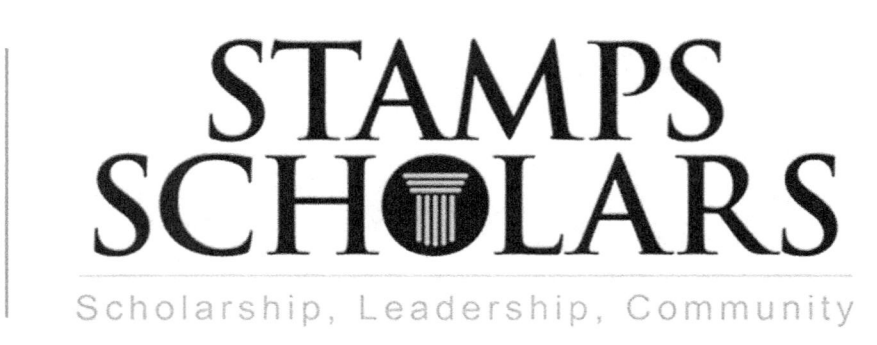

STAMPS SCHOLARS
Scholarship, Leadership, Community

OVERVIEW

The Stamps Scholars Program, with its partner schools, seeks students who demonstrate academic merit, strong leadership potential, and exceptional character.

The Stamps Scholars Program welcomes and supports students from all backgrounds and areas of study. Financial need is not a consideration. At some of the partner schools, international students are eligible for the Stamps Scholarship. Students should check directly with the program that they are interested in to view eligibility requirements.

If you are interested in being considered for a Stamps Scholarship, please contact one (or more) of the partner schools directly. Scholarships are awarded by the partner schools. Scholarship terms vary, so please check with the schools in which you are interested in for more details on how to apply and what the benefits of the award are at that college or university.

There are 37 Stamps Scholar partner schools across the **US** and into the **UK**.

Through partnerships with institutions across the U.S. (and into the U.K.), Scholars receive annual awards that range from $5,400 to $75,000 (four-year awards total an average of $21,600-$300,000) with additional funds for enrichment activities such as study abroad, academic conferences, and leadership training. The Stamps Scholars Program and partner schools evenly share the costs of the awards.

Stamps scholarship application deadline varies from one partner school to another. Please check with the schools you are interested in for more details on how to apply.

FULL RIDE EXTERNAL SCHOLARSHIPS

Frequently Asked Questions

When does the Stamps Scholars Program Application Open?

Stamps Scholarship application deadline varies from one partner school to another. Please check with the schools in which you are interested in more details on how to apply.

What does the Stamps Scholars Program Cover?

Through partnerships with institutions across the U.S. (and into the U.K.), Scholars receive annual awards that range from $5,400 to $75,000 (four-year awards total an average of $21,600-$300,000) with additional funds for enrichment activities such as study abroad, academic conferences, and leadership training.

The award value of the Stamps scholarship varies from one partner school to another.

In any case, most partner schools give awards of up to the full cost of undergraduate enrollment.

I am a current high school senior, am I eligible to apply?

An eligible student must be a candidate for high school graduation at the end of the current academic year, and plan to enroll in any Stamps partner schools.

Selection Criteria

Applying for a Stamps Scholarship is easy. A student must apply directly to one or more of the partner schools to be considered for the Stamps Scholarship. If you qualify, you'll automatically be considered for a Stamps award.

In some cases, however, some partner schools may request a separate application for consideration of the Stamps Scholarship.

At certain schools, the Stamps Scholarship Program is part of an umbrella program for scholars, such as the Foundation Fellows at the University of Georgia or the Carolina Scholars at the University of South Carolina.

Generally Top Applicants are selected!

How old is the Stamps Scholars Program?

The Stamps Scholars Program was founded by E. Roe Stamps and his late wife Penny in 2006, with the purpose of enabling extraordinary educational experiences for extraordinary students.

I'm an international student, am I eligible to apply for the Stamps Scholars Program?

Yes, at *some of the partner schools*, *international students* are eligible for the Stamps Scholarship.

View more Details and more information on the Stamps Scholars Scholarship Site.

☑ **Application Link: https://www.stampsscholars.org/**

Ingram Scholars Program

OVERVIEW

The Ingram Scholars Program challenges students to create and implement substantial service projects in the community. The program supports students who demonstrate a willingness and ability to combine a successful business or professional career with a lifelong commitment to finding solutions to critical problems facing modern society. Ingram Scholars are expected to devote approximately twenty hours each month during the academic year and at least one of their undergraduate summers to relevant community outreach and service projects.

Ingram Scholars receive full-tuition support each year plus a stipend for a special summer service project. Vanderbilt will provide additional need-based financial aid to those Ingram Scholarship recipients whose demonstrated financial need exceeds the amount of full tuition.

Ingram Scholars are selected on the basis of commitment to civic-minded service, an entrepreneurial spirit, strength of personal character, and leadership potential. In evaluating candidates, the selection committee reviews the Ingram Scholars Program application along with the entire application for first-year admission. Ingram Scholar Finalists are also required to interview with the selection committee.

The Ingram Scholars Program is a unique and innovative example of how a university can prepare students for responsible careers and a lifetime of useful contributions to the well-being of others. If you are committed to generating positive social change, and if you possess the qualities of maturity, leadership, and initiative, you should consider this challenging and rewarding program.

Ingram Scholars Program applications for prospective freshmen must be submitted electronically via your **MyAppVU** account by December 1.

FULL RIDE EXTERNAL SCHOLARSHIPS

Frequently Asked Questions

When does the Ingram Scholars Program Application Open?

Ingram Scholars Program applications for prospective freshmen must be submitted electronically via your MyAppVU account by December 1.

What does the Ingram Scholars Program Cover?

Ingram Scholars receive full-tuition support each year plus a stipend for a special summer service project. *Vanderbilt University* will provide additional need-based financial aid to those Ingram Scholarship recipients whose demonstrated financial need exceeds the amount of full tuition.

I am a current high school senior, am I eligible to apply?

An eligible student must be a candidate for high school graduation at the end of the current academic year, and plan to enroll in the Vanderbilt University.

Selection Criteria

The Ingram Scholars Program application is strongly encouraged; preference is given to those who apply. Applicants apply via MyAppVU after submitting admission application.

Ingram Scholars are selected on the basis of commitment to civic-minded service, an entrepreneurial spirit, strength of personal character, and leadership potential.

Generally Top Applicants are selected!

How old is the Ingram Scholars Program?

E. Bronson Ingram, chairman of the Vanderbilt University Board of Trust from 1991 until his death in 1995, conceived of the Ingram Scholars Program in 1993 as a way to encourage Vanderbilt students to combine a professional career with a commitment to community service.

I'm an international student, am I eligible to apply for the Ingram Scholars Program?

All applicants for first-year admission are eligible and considered for this scholarship.

View more Details and more information on the Ingram Scholars Program Scholarship Site.

☑ **Application Link: https://www.vanderbilt.edu/scholarships/ingram.php**

Evans Scholars Foundation

OVERVIEW

The Evans Scholarship is a full tuition and housing college scholarship for high-achieving caddies with limited financial means.

To qualify, caddies must meet the requirements of having a strong caddie record, excellent academics, demonstrated financial need and outstanding character.
Scholarship applications are accepted at the beginning of an applicant's senior year of high school, as well as from college freshmen.

This is the largest scholarship program for caddies in the United States. The program has helped thousands of hardworking young men and women get into college since 1930. The Evans Scholars Program addresses the barriers to college graduation faced by students and prepares them for a lifetime of success.

The Western Golf Association conducts championships for professional and amateur golfers, promotes the use of caddies and supports the Evans Scholars Foundation's efforts to award full tuition and housing college scholarships to hardworking caddies with limited financial means.

The entire application – including supporting documents like evaluations, recommendation letters, transcripts, test scores, a **CSS** profile and **FAFSA** information – is expected to be completed by October 30. The Scholarship Committee will begin its review when the application is complete.

FULL RIDE EXTERNAL SCHOLARSHIPS

Frequently Asked Questions

When does the Evans Scholarship Application Open?

Scholarship applications are accepted at the beginning of an applicant's senior year of high school, as well as from college freshmen. The entire application – including supporting documents like evaluations, recommendation letters, transcripts, test scores, a CSS profile and FAFSA information – must be completed by October 30.

What does the Evans Scholarship Cover?

The Evans Scholars Foundation is a charitable trust that provides full, four-year tuition and housing college scholarships to deserving caddies. The Foundation is overseen by the Western Golf Association, which also runs six prestigious golf tournaments, including the BMW Championship.

I am a current high school senior, am I eligible to apply?

Scholarship applications are accepted at the beginning of an applicant's senior year of high school, as well as from college freshmen. Most Scholarships are awarded during the applicant's senior year in high school. Applications are reviewed by the Scholarship Committee.

Selection Criteria

All applicants must possess the following requirements:

- ✓ Strong Caddie Record: Applicants must have caddied, regularly and successfully, for a minimum of two years and are expected to caddie at their sponsoring club the year they apply for the Scholarship.
- ✓ Excellent Academics: Applicants must have completed their junior year of high school with above a B average in college preparatory courses. SAT and ACT test scores are also required.
- ✓ Demonstrated Financial Need.
- ✓ An Outstanding Character.

How old is the Evans Scholarship?

In 1930, the Western Golf Association and celebrated amateur golfer Charles "Chick" Evans Jr. established the Evans Scholars Foundation. The Foundation's mission was to provide full tuition and college scholarships to caddies with limited financial means.

I'm an international student, am I eligible to apply for the Evans Scholarship?

To be an Evans Scholar, an applicant must be a US citizen or permanent resident.

View more Details and more information on the Evans Scholarship Site.

☑ **Application Link: https://www.wgaesf.org/**

Park Scholarship Program

NC STATE UNIVERSITY

Park Scholarships

OVERVIEW

The Park Scholarship Program provides a four-year, full ride scholarship to North Carolina State University. Awarded on the basis of outstanding accomplishments and potential in scholarship, leadership, service, and character.

The mission of the Park Scholarships program is to bring exceptional students to NC State, based on outstanding accomplishments and potential in scholarship, leadership, service, and character.

Park Scholars are intellectually curious students who think critically and seek learning experiences outside the classroom. They listen well, lead by example, take risks, and champion original ideas. Park Scholars dedicate themselves to making a positive difference in their communities while demonstrating integrity, honesty, and conscientiousness.

In addition to academic and professional pursuits, the Park Scholars engage in several team and class endeavors during their four years at NC State. They are creative, smart, motivated, service-oriented, and participate in a wide array of extracurricular activities, including student government, varsity and intramural athletics, fraternities and sororities, academic and cause-related clubs, entrepreneurial ventures, and arts organizations.

The Park Scholarships program is named for the late Roy H. Park an NC State alumnus who created the charitable Park Foundation, dedicated to education, media, and the environment.

Applicants should submit a complete Park Scholarships application by November 1.

FULL RIDE EXTERNAL SCHOLARSHIPS

Frequently Asked Questions

When does the Park Scholarship Application Open?

Applicants are advised to submit a complete Park Scholarships application by November 1. The application processes for Park Scholarships and NC State undergraduate admissions are separate, check site for more details on how to apply.

What does the Park Scholarship Cover?

Four-year scholarship valued at $116,000 for in-state students and $213,000 for out-of-state students, including tuition and fees, room and board, books and supplies, travel, and personal expenses. Grants to fund professional and personal enrichment experiences, such as research projects, service activities, and conferences in the United States and abroad. Guaranteed invitation to join the University Honors Program for all Park Scholarships Finalists.

I am a current high school senior, am I eligible to apply?

An eligible student should be applying for fall, first-year admission into a baccalaureate program at NC State University.

Selection Criteria

To be eligible for the Park Scholarships program, candidates **must** be United States citizens, permanent residents of the U.S., or graduating from a high school located in the U.S. (regardless of citizenship status)

Top applicants to the North Carolina State University are duly considered for this scholarship.
The Park Scholarships application asks that you provide:
Names and email addresses of two recommenders,
Information about advanced coursework completed and two essays.

How old is the Park Scholarship Program?

With a generous grant from the Park Foundation, the Park Scholarships program was established in 1996 to provide a superb educational opportunity for exceptionally talented and well-prepared young people who merit the intellectual challenge of a distinguished faculty and a superior university.

Can the Park Scholarship be deferred?

YES; in fact, students are encouraged to defer their university studies for one year to travel or work abroad or to engage in some other "gap year" activity. Incoming students may request a deferral in writing.

View more Details and more information on the Park Scholarship website.

☑ **Application Link: https://park.ncsu.edu/**

8. JP Morgan Chase & Co. : Thomas G. Labrecque Smart Start Program

OVERVIEW

Thomas G. Labrecque Smart Start Program is designed for ambitious, analytical New York City high school students who are willing to get a head start on a <u>career in financial services</u>.

If you're an ambitious, analytical New York City high school student who is ready to get a head start on a career in financial services, then Smart Start is the program for you. You'll gain real-world experience working in industry-leading businesses while attending university on a <u>full four-year scholarship</u>. Applicants will learn the skills needed for a successful career in financial services while working part-time during the school year and full-time during the summer. Each year, you'll rotate to another area of the firm as you expand your knowledge, learn about the variety of roles in financial services, and build the foundation for your future career.
The thrilling part is you'll do all of this on a full four-year scholarship to an approved college or university.

Applicant must be a graduating senior from a New York City high school who is a New York City resident that has been accepted to one of the following colleges: Barnard College, Baruch College, Brooklyn College, City College, Columbia University, Fordham University (Lincoln Center campus, Rosehill campus), Long Island University (Brooklyn campus), New York University, Pace University (Manhattan campus), Polytechnic Institute of New York University, St. Francis College, or St. John's University.
Three essays and recommendations required. Financial need and community involvement must be demonstrated.

P.S: Life science or fine art majors are not eligible for this scholarship.

The deadline for this scholarship is January 17.

FULL RIDE EXTERNAL SCHOLARSHIPS

Frequently Asked Questions

When does the Thomas G. Labrecque Smart Start Program Application Open?

The deadline for this scholarship is usually in January of each year.

What does the Thomas G. Labrecque Smart Start Program Cover?

This is a full tuition scholarship that also includes a yearly stipend for books and supplies and four years of paid internship with J.P. Morgan Chase which includes: Specific work assignments, On-the-job training, A support network of mentors, peer advisors and a Smart Start program to assist in assimilation into a corporate environment, plus other benefits.

I am a current high school senior, am I eligible to apply?

Applicant must be a graduating senior from a New York City high school who is a New York City resident that has been accepted to an approved college or university.

I'm an international student, am I eligible to apply for the Thomas G. Labrecque Smart Start Program?

Applicant must be a New York City resident who attends a public, parochial or private high school in one of NYC's five boroughs.

Selection Criteria

Applicants must rank in the top 90 percent of their class and have SAT/ACT scores (minimum 1000 combined for verbal and math, and 21. for ACT.)

Applicant must have an interest in *financial services* as well as the discipline to simultaneously pursue their education and work in a fast-paced environment. You should be flexible, adaptable, detail oriented, have good judgment and the ability to manage multiple responsibilities.

P.S: Applicant must be a graduating senior from a New York City high school who is a New York City resident.

How old is the Thomas G. Labrecque Smart Start Program?

The J.P. Morgan Thomas G. Labrecque Smart Start Program, which annually offers New York City students a full-tuition scholarship, four years of rotational internships, a mentoring network and professional at any of 11 NYC universities, was originally created by Labrecque in 1992.

View more Details and more information on the Thomas G. Labrecque Smart Start Program website.

☑ **Application Link:**

https://careers.jpmorgan.com/us/en/students/programs/smart-start

Bruce Fishkin Scholarship Fund

BRUCE FISHKIN SCHOLARSHIP FUND
Ability Is Nothing without Opportunity

OVERVIEW

The Bruce Fishkin Scholarship fund awards up to the entire cost of a college education to outstanding students believed to deserve an investment of the time and money.

Awards are not based upon need, but rather on ability, individuality, and potential. If you have always known deep inside that given the chance, you'd achieve greatness, well, here is that chance.

The scholarship fund is in search of high school students in their senior year who seek to challenge themselves to succeed and accomplish what most people never imagine. Selection is based upon application essays, followed by personal interviews.

The scholarship board anticipates awarding scholarships annually to students that either reside or attend high school in any one of the following areas: Fairfield, Greens Farms, Redding and Westport, Connecticut and the cities and surrounding suburbs of Chicago, Illinois and Las Vegas, Nevada.

P.S: Only students from the United States are eligible to apply for this scholarship. You can also be eligible for this scholarship if you are a **US Permanent Resident** residing in the catchment area of the scholarship.

Applications for this scholarship may be submitted beginning **Sept 1st at 12:00 PM**, and will be accepted until **October 17th at 11:59 AM**.

FULL RIDE EXTERNAL SCHOLARSHIPS

Frequently Asked Questions

When does the Bruce Fishkin Scholarship Application Open?

Applications for the Bruce Fishkin scholarship may be submitted beginning Sept 1, and will be accepted until October 17.

What does the Bruce Fishkin Scholarship Cover?

The Bruce Fishkin Scholarship fund awards up to the entire cost of a college education to outstanding students. The scholarships are awarded in various amounts, up to a "full ride". The scholarship can be used for up to 8 semesters for undergraduate education. Funding can be used to pay for tuition, room and board, books, supplies and equipment that are required based on your course syllabus.

P.S: Students may transfer from one institution to another and retain the award.

I am a current high school senior, am I eligible to apply?

Applicant must be entering his or her senior year of high school in the fall of the application year, or have finished senior year of high school in the current application year.

Selection Criteria

Applicant must be a resident or attend high school in any one of the following areas: Chicago, Illinois or the counties of Cook, DuPage, Kane, Lake, McHenry or Will, Illinois – Las Vegas, Nevada and suburbs of the area – Fairfield, Greens Farms, Redding or Westport, Connecticut.

A minimum high school GPA of 3.0 on a 4.0 scale, or the equivalent thereof in cases where the applicable high school does not employ a traditional 4.0 system.

A minimum ACT score of 22 OR a minimum SAT score of 1100.

Plan on attending an accredited college or university for a Bachelor's degree or four-year program in the United States.

How old is the Bruce Fishkin Scholarship?

Formed in 2010, the Fund will award up to the entire cost of a college education to outstanding students.

I'm an international student, am I eligible to apply for the Bruce Fishkin Scholarship?

Only students from the United States or Permanent Resident residing in the catchment area(s) are eligible to apply for this scholarship.

View more Details and more information on the Bruce Fishkin Scholarship application website.

☑ **Application Link:** https://brucefishkinscholarshipfund.com/

10. National Merit Scholarship Program

OVERVIEW

The **National Merit Scholarship Program** is an academic competition for recognition and scholarships that began in 1955. Approximately 1.5 million high school students enter the program each year. It is one of the largest scholarship programs in the United States.

Since its founding, the National Merit Scholarship Program has recognized over 3.4 million students and provided some 451,000 scholarships worth over $1.8 billion. The honors awarded by **NMSC** to exceptionally able students are viewed as definitive marks of excellence.

Merit Scholarship awards are of three types:

- **National Merit $2500 Scholarships** – Every finalist competes for these single-payment scholarships, which are awarded on a state-representational basis. Winners are selected by a committee of college admission officers and high school counselors without consideration of family financial circumstances, college choice, or major and career plans.
- **Corporate-sponsored Merit Scholarship Awards** – Corporate sponsors designate their awards for children of their employees or members, for residents of a community where a company has operations, or for Finalists with career plans the sponsor wishes to encourage.
- **College-sponsored Merit Scholarship Awards** – Officials of each sponsor college select winners of their awards from Finalists who have been accepted for admission and have informed NMSC by the published deadlines that the sponsor college or university is their first choice. These awards are renewable for up to four years of undergraduate study.

Please refer back to the Full ride section and check out for schools (i.e. *College-sponsored Merit Scholarship awards*) that offer Full ride scholarships to National Merit Finalists.

FULL RIDE EXTERNAL SCHOLARSHIPS

Frequently Asked Questions

When does the National Merit Scholarship Program Application Open?

Applicants should refer back to the **Full ride section** and check out for schools (i.e. *Full Institutional Scholarships*) that offer Full ride scholarships to National Merit Finalists. Application details of each College or University sponsor are listed under the respective College's and Universities.

What does the National Merit Scholarship Program Cover?

College-sponsored Merit Scholarship awards, mostly offer Full ride Scholarships to National Merit Finalist. Please refer back to the Full ride institutional scholarships and check out for Universities and Colleges that offer Full ride scholarships to National Merit Finalists.

I am a current high school senior, am I eligible to apply?

To enter the competition, a high school student must take the PSAT/NMSQT® at a local high school or approved location in the specified year of high school and meet NMSC's published program participation requirements.

Student Entry Requirements

Candidates should take the PSAT/NMSQT in the specified year of the high school program and no later than the third year in grades 9 through 12.

Attend high school in the United States, the District of Columbia, or U.S. commonwealth and territory; or meet the citizenship requirements for students attending high school outside the United States (check site for more details).

Typically, all interested candidates that meet the student entry requirements are eligible to participate in the competition.

How old is the National Merit Scholarship Program?

Established in 1955, National Merit Scholarship Corporation (NMSC®) is an independent, not-for-profit organization that operates without government assistance.

I'm an international student, am I eligible to apply for the National Merit Scholarship Program?

To be eligible for the Scholarship program, candidates **must** be United States citizens, permanent residents of the U.S., or graduating from a high school located in the U.S. (regardless of citizenship status)

View more Details and more information on the National Merit Scholarship Program website.

☑ **Application Link: https://www.nationalmerit.org/**

Johnson Scholarship

OVERVIEW

Washington and Lee University offers the Johnson Scholarship Program which selects students on the basis of academic achievement, demonstrated leadership and their potential to contribute to the intellectual and civic life of the W&L campus and of the world at large in years to come.

The Johnson Scholarship recipients receive awards of at least tuition, room and board to attend Washington and Lee University. Students with financial needs higher than this amount will have any additional needs met by the scholarship. In addition, Johnson Scholars receive funding up to $7,000 to support summer experiences during their time at W&L.

Finalists for Johnson Scholarships participate in an on-campus competition and are notified in late March of their status. All costs associated with attending the competition will be paid by Washington and Lee University, including travel expenses (airfare or mileage costs), meals and lodging for the duration of the competition.

Students who wish to be considered for a Johnson Scholarship must submit a complete Common App, including the additional Johnson Scholarship application essay, no later than December 1.

P.S: All Johnson Scholarship application instructions are included in W&L's section of the Common App.

FULL RIDE EXTERNAL SCHOLARSHIPS

Frequently Asked Questions

When does the Johnson Scholarship Program Application Open?

Students who wish to be considered for a Johnson Scholarship must submit application no later than December 1.

What does the Johnson Scholarship Program Cover?

Recipients of the Johnson Scholarship receive awards of at **least tuition, room and board** to attend Washington and Lee University.
Students with financial need higher than this amount will have any additional need met by the scholarship.
In addition, Johnson Scholars receive funding up to **$7,000 to support summer experiences** during their time at W&L.

I am a current high school senior, am I eligible to apply?

Johnson Scholarships are awarded to approximately 10% of each entering class at Washington and Lee University.

I'm an international student, am I eligible to apply for the Johnson Scholarship Program?

All applicants for first-year admission are automatically considered for this scholarship.

Selection Criteria

A complete application consists of:

- A complete Common App, including the Johnson Scholarship Application essay.
- An official copy of your high school transcript.
- Self-reported or official scores from the SAT or ACT
- Two teacher recommendations.
- One school counsellor recommendation and secondary school form.

Applicants should demonstrate potential for stellar academic performance. Top applicants to Washington and Lee University are duly considered for this scholarship.

How old is the Johnson Scholarship Program?

The Johnson Scholarship program was established in 2007 as a result of an historic $100 million gift to Washington and Lee.

I am a current high school senior intending to take a gap year before beginning college, am I eligible to apply?

Yes, all applicants for first-year admission are automatically considered for this scholarship regardless of your background.

View more Details and more information on the Johnson Scholarship website.

☑ **Application Link: https://my.wlu.edu/the-johnson-program**

Alfond Scholars Program

Alfond Scholarship Foundation

OVERVIEW

The Alfond Scholars Programs annually awards full ride scholarships – including tuition, double room, and unlimited board – to entering first-year students in the College of Liberal Arts at Rollins College with the desire and commitment to pursue additional prestigious recognition such as Rhodes, Goldwater, or Truman scholarships during their undergraduate years. Scholarship totals include federal and state awards for which a student might already be eligible. Alfond Scholarships are renewable for three additional years, bringing the value of each scholarship to more than $280,000 over four years.

Scholarship recipients will be identified from the fall applicant pool on the basis of strength of selection criteria. A select number of qualified applicants will be invited to the Scholars Weekend interview competition which will introduce students to the extraordinary benefits of being a scholar at Rollins. The academic competition portion of the weekend will consist of a mock classroom experience and individual and group interviews with Rollins faculty, staff, and students.

Scholarship finalists are selected from the College of Liberal Arts applicant pool. All admission applicants who submit all application materials by the Priority Scholarship Deadline (Nov. 15) are considered for Alfond Scholarships on the basis of their overall academic record.

FULL RIDE EXTERNAL SCHOLARSHIPS

Frequently Asked Questions

When does the Alfond Scholarship Application Open?

Applications for this scholarship will end on November 15. All admission applicants are advised to submit all application materials by this priority scholarship deadline.

What does the Alfond Scholars Program Cover?

The Alfond Scholars Program awards Full Scholarships – including tuition, double room, and unlimited board – to entering first-year students in the College of Liberal Arts at Rollins College.

Alfond Scholars join an exceptional group of Rollins students who are mentored as candidates for intellectual academic recognition as Rhodes, Truman, and Goldwater scholars, and as recipients of other prestigious awards.

I am a current high school senior, am I eligible to apply?

An eligible applicant must be an entering first year student in the College of Liberal Arts at Rollins College.

I'm an international student, am I eligible to apply for the Alfond Scholars Program?

All applicants for first-year admission are automatically considered for this scholarship.

Selection Criteria

Scholarship finalists are selected from the College of Liberal Arts applicant pool.

Qualifying applicants typically have SATs higher than 1450 (Evidence Based Reading and Math) or ACTs higher than 32 (Composite) and GPAs higher than 3.8. Test-optional students are considered as well.
Strength of high school curriculum and extracurricular involvement are also important factors.

Opportunities & Obligations

- Participation and completion of Rollins Honors Degree Program.
- Mentoring by Rollins Office of External and Competitive Scholarships and the Associate Dean of Advising
- Enrollment in the intersession service Immersion course during the first year.
- Participation in at least one off-campus experience such as Washington semester or study abroad during the first three years
- Maintaining 3.33 GPA
- Living on campus for four years.

View more Details and more information on the Alfond Scholarship website.

☑ **Application Link:** https://www.rollins.edu/financial-aid/as-cps-financial-aid/scholarships/alfond-scholars-program.html

Cunniffe Presidential Scholarship

OVERVIEW

The Maurice J. and Carolyn Dursi Cunniffe Presidential Scholarship is awarded to entering traditional first-year students who generally rank in the top 1 to 2 percent in their high school class.

The award covers tuition, room, board, and fees and is renewable for four years. Recipients are also eligible for a maximum of $20,000 over four years to use for academic enrichment experiences.

This scholarship is awarded by Fordham University. The scholarship is awarded on the basis of excellent academic achievement in high school, test scores and personal characteristics.

Fordham University is devoted to the transmission of learning, through research and through undergraduate, graduate, and professional education of the highest quality. It encourages the growth of a life of faith consonant with moral and intellectual development.

The **Cunniffe Presidential Scholars** are generally ranked in the top 1-2% of their high school class and represent the most talented students as demonstrated by their outstanding academic performance, personal characteristics, as well as their commitment, leadership, and service.

The deadline is typically in March. Award recipients will be selected by mid-April.

FULL RIDE EXTERNAL SCHOLARSHIPS

Frequently Asked Questions

When does the Cunniffe Presidential Scholars Program Application Open?

The deadline for application is usually in March. Award recipients will be selected by mid-April.

What does the Cunniffe Presidential Scholars Program Cover?

The award covers tuition, room, board, and fees and is renewable for four years. Recipients are also eligible for a maximum of $20,000 over four years to use for academic enrichment experiences.

I am a current high school senior, am I eligible to apply?

The Cunniffe Presidential Scholarship is awarded to entering traditional first-year students into Fordham University.

I'm an international student, am I eligible to apply for the Cunniffe Presidential Scholars Program?

All applicants for first-year admission are automatically considered for this scholarship.

International students are very much eligible for this scholarship.

Selection Criteria

The Cunniffe Presidential Scholarship is awarded to entering traditional first-year students who generally rank in the top 1 to 2 percent in their high school class.

Top applicants to Fordham University are duly considered for this scholarship.

How old is the Cunniffe Presidential Scholars Program?

Founded in 1841, Fordham University is the third-oldest university in New York State composed of four undergraduate and six graduate schools. It strives for excellence in research and teaching, and prepares students for leadership in a global society.

How to Apply

To apply for this scholarship, applicants must be admitted in an undergraduate degree program at Fordham University.
After being registered, candidates will be automatically considered for this education award.
P.S: If your high school education has not been conducted in the English language, you will be expected to demonstrate evidence of an adequate level of English proficiency.

Candidates must submit a CV, academic certificates, and transcripts with your application.

View more Details and more information on the Cunniffe Presidential Scholars Program website.

☑ **Application Link:** https://www.Fordham.edu/undergraduate-admission/apply/scholarships-and-grants/

Belk Scholarship

OVERVIEW

The John M. Belk Scholarship provides comprehensive funding (tuition, fees, room and board) plus special study stipends that allow you greater flexibility in the on-and off-campus opportunities you choose to explore. Those experiences, paired with the academic programs, deepen your intellect, maturity, and global understanding.

Nomination & Selection Process:
Applicants are required to be nominated by their high school Guidance counsellors, heads of school, or principals. One or two candidates may be nominated from each school.
The admission staff may also nominate students based on the strength of their application for admission.

The John M. Belk Scholarship is awarded at Davidson College in Davidson, North Carolina.

The Program is built around a belief that, as a Belk Scholar, you possess unique talents that should be recognized and nurtured.

A candidate's record and recommendations must demonstrate academic excellence and purposeful engagement in the classroom, in student and civic organizations, on the athletic field, or in the arts. While academic achievement is paramount, Belk Scholars also exhibit intellectual curiosity and a commitment to both their local and global communities.

Nominations must be made by December 1 by completing the online nomination form and submitting the required documentation (recommendation letter and transcript) to Admission and Financial Aid.

FULL RIDE EXTERNAL SCHOLARSHIPS

Frequently Asked Questions

When does the Belk Scholarship Application Open?

Nominations must be made by December 1 by completing the online nomination form and submitting the required documentation to Admission and Financial Aid Office.

Application completion deadline for nominees is typically by December 15.

View Davidson's application options and learn more about applying to Davidson.

What does the Belk Scholarship Program Cover?

The John M. Belk Scholarship provides comprehensive funding (tuition, fees, room and board) plus special study stipends that allow you greater flexibility in the on-and off-campus opportunities you choose to explore.

I am a current high school senior, am I eligible to apply?

An eligible student must be a candidate for high school graduation at the end of the current academic year, and plan to enroll in Davidson's College.

Selection Criteria

This is a nomination Scholarship.
Guidance counselors, heads of school, or principals may nominate one or two candidates from each school. The admission staff may also nominate students based on the strength of their application for admission.

Typically, candidates with high grades are nominated for this scholarship.

How old is the Belk Scholarship Program?

In the early 1990s, the John Montgomery Belk Scholarship was established, following up with an historic gift in 2000 to endow the program. Today, it is one of the most prestigious and generous undergraduate scholarships in the United States.

I'm an international student, am I eligible to apply for the Belk Scholarship Program?

Yes, Davidson College invites high schools from across the country and *abroad* to nominate outstanding students with extraordinary potential to compete for the John M. Belk Scholarship.

View more Details and more information on the Belk Scholarship Program website.

☑ **Application Link:** https://www.davidson.edu/admission-and-financial-aid/financial-aid/scholarships

Wells Scholar Program

WELLS SCHOLARS PROGRAM

OVERVIEW

The Wells Scholar Program created in honor of Herman B Wells, 11th President of the University of Indiana, is one of the most competitive and prestigious awards offered by an American University. The Wells Scholars Program guarantees the full cost of attendance for four years of undergraduate study on IU's Bloomington campus.

The Wells Scholars Program uses a nomination rather than an application process for the selection of scholars.
Each year, selected incoming freshmen to the University of Indiana receive the award, based solely on merit. In addition, one to two current IUB students are selected to join the junior or senior class of Scholars.
Wells Scholars are also members of the Hutton Honors College, where they can apply for grants in support of research, internships, creative activity, conference travel, and honors thesis work.

The ideals of the Wells Scholar Program are not interested in students who see a brilliant career as their primary goal, they are interested in scholars who want to contribute and make an impact on their community, the nation, and the world at large.

The deadline for receipt of fully completed electronic nominations and supplementary materials, including letters of recommendation and student essays is by November 1. Complete nominations that include all required items must be submitted through the online portal.

FULL RIDE EXTERNAL SCHOLARSHIPS

Frequently Asked Questions

When does the Wells Scholar Program Application Open?

Nomination information is emailed to all eligible high schools by early August. Students who are not selected by their schools or who otherwise wish to be nominated should follow the instructions on the *Domestic High School Senior Nomination Process page*.

Check site for more details

The deadline for receipt of fully completed electronic nominations and supplementary materials, including letters of recommendation and student essays is by November 1.

What does the Wells Scholar Program Cover?

The Wells Scholars Program guarantees the full cost of attendance for a period of eight semesters of undergraduate study at Indiana University Bloomington. The award includes Full tuition and mandatory and course-related fees for a standard course load of 12-18 credits, as well as a living stipend during the fall and spring sufficient to cover the cost of a standard double dorm room contract and a standard meal plan in the residence halls.

P.S: Students receive the same stipend whether they choose to live on or off campus.

Selection Criteria

There is no strict model of an award recipient: however, past successful nominees have typically;

- ✓ Shown exceptional qualities of character and leadership
- ✓ Been significantly involved in extracurricular activities
- ✓ Demonstrated a concern for their community
- ✓ Excelled in terms of class rank, GPA, and/or (optional) standardized test scores
- ✓ Expressed interest in joining a community of scholarly individuals with diverse interests beyond a pre-professional track.

In addition to a pattern of serious commitment to one or more activities outside of class, past successful nominees generally place in the top 5% by class rank, have a GPA of at least 3.9 out of 4.0, and (optionally) a 1430+ SAT score and/or 32+ ACT score.

I'm an international student, am I eligible to apply for the Wells Scholar Program?

Yes, all nominated applicants for first-year admission are considered for this scholarship.

View more Details and more information on the Wells Scholar Program website.

☑ **Application Link: https://wellsscholars.indiana.edu/**

16 THE COOLIDGE SCHOLARSHIP

OVERVIEW

The Collidge Scholarship is awarded annually, it covers the student's tuition, room, board, and expenses for four years of undergraduate study.

It may be used at any accredited college or university in the United States.

Scholars from any background, pursuing any academic discipline of study may apply to this unbiased and need-blind program.

Requirements: Good academic achievement, extracurricular record and excellence in character.

Students apply for the Coolidge Scholarship during their junior year of high school. Finalists are flown in for a finalist weekend at the Coolidge Historic Site in Plymouth Notch, Vermont where they interview with the Coolidge Scholars Finalist Jury.

This Scholarship is in honor of Calvin Coolidge, the 30th President of the United States of America. He served from August 2, 1923 to March 4, 1929.

Calvin Coolidge worked hard in academics; the young New Englander's only sport was public speaking, often on public policy. The main criterion that distinguishes Coolidge Scholars therefore is academic excellence. Secondary criteria include: demonstrated interest in public policy; an appreciation for the values Coolidge championed; as well as humility and service.

The deadline for this scholarship is usually around January 26th Annually.

FULL RIDE EXTERNAL SCHOLARSHIPS

Frequently Asked Questions

When does the Coolidge Scholarship Application Open?

The Coolidge scholarship application opens around late summer yearly and the deadline is usually in late January.

When does the Coolidge Scholarship Cover?

A Coolidge Scholarship is among the most generous college scholarships available in the world. It covers a student's full tuition, room and board, and required fess for four years of undergraduate study. The Coolidge Scholarship also provides an annual stipend for books and supplies.

How old is the Coolidge Scholars Program?

The Coolidge Scholars Program launched in the winter of 2016 and the inaugural class was formally inducted in July 2016.

I'm an international student, am I eligible to apply for the Coolidge Scholarship?

The Coolidge Scholarship is only open to U.S. citizens and legal permanent residents. U.S. citizens or legal permanent residents currently attending high school abroad are indeed eligible to apply.

Selection Criteria

Primary Criterion: Academic Excellence

Secondary Criteria:
- Interest in Public Policy and Appreciation of Coolidge Values
- Humility and Service.

The Coolidge Scholarship is non-partisan and is awarded on merit regardless of race, gender, or background.

I am a current high school senior, am I eligible to apply?

No, only current high school juniors intending to enroll as undergraduates full-time for the first time in fall 2024 are eligible to apply for the 2023 scholarship. No exceptions to this rule can be made.

I am a current high school senior intending to take a gap year before beginning college, am I eligible to apply?

No, only current high school juniors are eligible to apply. No exceptions to this rule can be made.

View more Frequently Asked Questions (FAQs) and more information on the Coolidge Scholarship website.

☑ **Application Link:** https://coolidgescholars.org/

17 USDA 1890 NATIONAL SCHOLARS PROGRAM

OVERVIEW

The **USDA/1890 National Scholars Program** was established in 1992 as part of the partnership between the U.S. Department of Agriculture and the 1890 Land-Grant Universities.

The goal is to increase the the number of minorities studying agriculture, food, natural resource sciences, and the related disciplines.

Furthermore, the **USDA/1890 National Scholars Program** will provide full tuition, employment, employee benefits, fees, books, and room and board for up to 4 years to selected students. It is available for only bachelor's degree.

The scholarships are awarded annually and must be used at one of the 1890 Historically Black Land-Grant Universities. Also, the scholarship may be renewed each year, contingent upon satisfactory academic performance and normal progress toward the bachelor's degree.

The deadline for this scholarship is usually around January 15th Annually.

Frequently Asked Questions

Who Should Apply for the USDA/1890 National Scholars Program?

The USDA/1890 National Scholars Program is available to high school seniors entering their freshman year of college and rising sophomores and juniors.

What does the USDA/1890 Scholarship Cover?

This is one of the most generous Scholarship programs focused on, but not only for the black community. It covers a student's full tuition, room and board, and required fees for four years of undergraduate study. The Scholarship also covers fees, books and provides employment plus employment benefits.

How old is the USDA/1890 Scholars Program?

The Program was established in 1992.

I'm an international student, am I eligible to apply for the USDA/1890 Scholarship?

Unfortunately, international students are not qualified to apply for this scholarship. The eligibility requirement clearly states that student must be a U.S. Citizen.

General Eligibility Requirements

Interested candidates must meet the following requirements:

- Be a U.S. Citizen.
- Have a cumulative GPA of 3.0 or better (on a 4.0 scale)
- Have been accepted for admission or currently attending on of the nineteen 1890 Historically Black Land-Grant Universities
- Study agriculture, food, natural resouces sciences, or other related academic disciplines.
- Demonstrate leadership and community service
- Submit an official transcript with the school seal and an authorized official's signature
- Submit a signed application (original signature only)
- 21 ACT, 1080 SAT scores.

FULL RIDE EXTERNAL SCHOLARSHIPS

Frequently Asked Questions

The Nineteen 1890 Historically Black Land-Grant Universities, where the scholarships are offered:

- Alabama A&M University
- Alcorn State University, Mississippi
- Central State University, Ohio
- Delaware State University
- Florida A&M University
- Fort Valley State University, Georgia
- Kentucky State University
- Langston University, Oklahoma
- Lincoln University, Missouri
- North Carolina A&T State University
- Prairie View A&M University, Texas
- South Carolina State University
- Southern University, Louisiana
- Tennessee State University
- Tuskegee University, Alabama
- University of Arkansas Pine Bluff
- University of Maryland Eastern Shore
- Virginia State University
- West Virginia State University

National Scholars are required to study the following or related disciplines:

- Agriculture
- Agricultural Business/Management
- Agricultural Economics
- Agricultural Engineering/Mechanics
- Agricultural Production and Technology
- Agronomy or Crop Science
- Animal Sciences
- Botany
- Food Sciences/Technology
- Forestry and Related Sciences
- Home Economics/Nutrition
- Horticulture
- Natural Resources Management
- Soil Conservation/Soil Science
- Farm and Range Management
- Other related disciplines, (e.g. non-medical biological sciences, pre-veterinary medicine, computer science)

View more Frequently Asked Questions (FAQs) and further information on the USDA/1890 National Scholars program website.

☑ **Application Link:**
https://www.usda.gov/partnerships/1890NationalScholars

CAMERON IMPACT SCHOLARSHIP

OVERVIEW

The Cameron Impact Scholarship is a four-year, full-tuition (plus fees, and books) impact-driven undergraduate scholarship awarded annually. It may be used at any accredited college or university in the United States.

The scholarship is targetted at exceptional high school student who have demonstrated excellence in leadership, community service, extracurricular activities and academics.

As a merit-based program, the Cameron Impact Scholarship is open to all applicants who meet the **GPA** and citizenship requirements, regardless of race, socioeconomic status, religion, sexual orientation or any other background factors.

The Bryan Cameron Education Foundation is a private family foundation established in 2015 on the principle of making a difference by investing in young people's education. Their specific intent is to identify a select group of outstanding rising college students each year who we expect to positively impact the lives of their family, friends, colleagues, and fellow citizens.

Founder Bryan Cameron has enjoyed a long and successful career in asset management. His recognition and appreciation of his own blessings has inspired his extensive philanthropic initiatives over the years.

The Bryan Cameron Education Foundation core values are: Impact | Choice | Diversity | Higher Education | Merit | Service | and Accountability.

The deadline for this scholarship is usually around May 20th (Early) & September 9th (Regular) -- Both Annually.

Frequently Asked Questions

Who is eligible to apply to the Cameron Impact Scholarship?

US Citizens who have an unweighted GPA of 3.7 or higher are eligible to apply. The foundation is specifically looking for candidates who have displayed strong evidence of leadership, involvement in extracurriculars and community service, and who want to make a positive impact on the world around them.

What does the Cameron Impact Scholarship Cover?

This scholarship covers a student's full tuition, fees and books for four years of undergraduate study. The Cameron Scholarship also provides an annual stipend for books and supplies.

How old is the Cameron Impact Scholarship?

The Cameron Impact Scholarship was launched in the year 2015.

What if I am planning to do a gap year between high school and college?

Applicants who wish to take a gap year are welcome to apply to the Cameron Impact Scholarship. However, you should apply with the graduating high school class that you would be attending your first year of college with. So if you were to take a gap year, apply by May or September of your gap year. Describing what you have done in your gap year is an added advantage.

Will I be notified of my status even if I am not selected for an interview?

The Foundation notifies all Applicants of their status, regardless of if they receive a Finalist interview or not. Ensure to check your entire inbox including SPAM. Also, you are welcome to contact admin@bryancamronef.org to inquireabout the status of your Application.

May I submit my transcript or recommendations after the deadline?

The deadlines are hard ones, and any incomplete Applications will NOT be reviewed. Late submission of any Transcripts or Recommendations is not accepted. If any information is missing for the Early Application Deadline - your submission will automatically roll to the Regular Applicant Pool.

View more Frequently Asked Questions (FAQs) and more information on the Cameron Impact Scholarship website.

☑ **Application Link:**
https://www.bryancameroneducationfoundation.org/

19. THE GATES SCHOLARSHIP (TGS)

OVERVIEW

The Gates Scholarship (TGS) is a highly selective, last-dollar scholarship for outstanding, minority, high school seniors from low-income households. Each year, the scholarship is awarded to exceptional student leaders, with the intent of helping them realize their maximum potential.

It may be used at any **US** accredited, four-year, not-for-profit, private or public college or university. The institution must be based in the **US** or United States territory.

Scholars will receive funding for the full cost of attendance that is not already covered by other financial aid and the expected family contribution, as determined by the Free Application for Federal Student Aid (**FAFSA**), or the methodology used by a Scholar's college or university.

Cost of Attendance = tuition, fees, room, board, books, and transportation, and may include other personal costs.

The Gates Scholarship Program was launched in 2017. The Bill & Melinda Gates Foundation continues its long-standing commitment to helping outstanding minority students who come from low-income backgrounds realize their maximum potential.

This prestigious scholarship program is based on evidence that by eliminating the financial barriers to college, a last-dollar scholarship can enable high-potential, low-income minority students to excel in their course work, graduate college, and continue to be leaders throughout their lives.

The deadline for this scholarship is usually around January 15th Annually

FULL RIDE EXTERNAL SCHOLARSHIPS

Frequently Asked Questions

At what grade level are students eligible to apply? Must they be high school seniors?

The application is only open to high school seniors.

What does the Gates Scholarship Cover?

A very magnanimous scholarship indeed. It covers a student's full tuition, room and board, books, and required fees for four years of undergraduate study.

Can The Gates Scholarship be used for any major?

Yes. There are no restrictions on major or field of study. The program funds the completion of a bachelor's degree in the scholar's choice of major. It can also be used at any school of choice, provided the school is recognized/accredited.

Are there restrictions on the institutions a student can attend?

Unfortunately, international students are *not* qualified to apply for this scholarship. The eligibility requirement clearly states that student(s) must be a U.S. Citizen.

Who is eligible to apply for The Gates Scholarship?

To apply, students must be:
- A high school senior
- From at least one of the following ethnicities: African American, American Indian/Alaska Native, Asian & Pacific Islander American, and/or Hispanic American
- Pell-eligible
- A US citizen, national, or permanent resident
- In good academic standing with a minimum cumulative weighted GPA of 3.3 on a 4.0 scale (or equivalent)

Additionally, a student must plan to enroll full-time, in a four-year degree program, at a US accredited, not-for-profit, private or public college or university.

For American Indian/Alaska Native, proof of tribal enrollment will be required.

What is Pell-eligibility?

Pell-eligibility is calculated by the U.S. Department of Education after a student submits the Free Application for Federal Student Aid (FAFSA). It is based on family contribution, status as a full-time student, and the student's academic plans. The household income of Pell-eligible students varies. In recent years, 99% of Pell-eligible students came from households with incomes of $80,000 or less per year.

View more Frequently Asked Questions (FAQs) and more information visit the Gates Scholarship website.

☑ **Application Link: https://www.thegatesscholarship.org/**

20 QUESTBRIDGE NATIONAL COLLEGE MATCH WITH FULL RIDE SCHOLARSHIPS

QUESTBRIDGE

QuestBridge National College Match Scholarships

OVERVIEW

The **QuestBridge National College Match** is targeted at low-income high school seniors who have excelled academically, but are financial disadvantaged.

These students will be matched with top colleges and considered for early admisssion and full four-year scholarships. Questbridge partners with over 30 colleges and universities that will offer full ride scholarships to these students.

The full scholarship covers tuition, fees, room & board, other expenses. It may be used at any of the 30+ questbridge college(s) or universities.

Over 10,500 students have been admitted with full four-year scholarships. Students who attend the partner colleges are supported in their college years and beyond through on-campus chapters and nationwide opportunities offered through the **QuestBridge Scholars Network and QuestBridge Alumni Association.**

QuestBridge grew from a few simple ideas and a lot of help along the way. With roots extending to 1987.

The Quest Scholars Program officially started in 1994 as a five-week residential summer enrichment program for high school juniors on Stanford University's campus. After the summer session, Quest provided five years of academic and personal support to our students. Ten years later in 2004, Quest launched QuestBridge in an effort to expand the number of high school students it reached.

The deadline for this scholarship is usually around September 27th Annually.

FULL RIDE EXTERNAL SCHOLARSHIPS

Frequently Asked Questions

Who is the National College Match for?

QuestBridge programs are open to students of all races, ethnicities, and cultural backgrounds. They recognize that students of all backgrounds may face financial and circumstantial obstacles to higher education. They look for low-income students who have excelled academically.

Please visit https://www.questbridge.org/high-school-students/national-college-match/who-should-apply – For more info.

What does QuestBridge consider low-income?

Most of the students who are selected as Finalists come from households earning less than $65,000 per year for a typical family of four with minimal significant assets. However, there are no absolute cut-offs. If a student comes from a household earning more than this amount but feels that they have faced economic hardship and fit the QuestBridge criteria of high-achieving, low-income students, we would encourage that student to apply. There is room on the application to explain the family's situation.

Can I apply to the National College Match if I am not a U.S. Citizen or Permanent Resident?

The QuestBridge National College Match is open to all:
U.S. Citizens and Permanent Residents
Students, regardless of citizenship, currently attending a high school in the United States.

Learn more:
https://questbridge.zendesk.com/hc/en-us/articles/218776877

What does QuestBridge consider high-achieving?

QuestBridge Finalists are motivated students who challenge themselves by taking and excelling in their high school's most rigorous courses. Questbridge, as well as their college partners, look at many different factors when assessing a student's academics, including grades, class rank, high school courses taken, standardized test scores (if taken), writing ability, teacher recommendations, School Report (also known as the counselor recommendation) and other markers of talent and motivation.

Learn more:
https://www.questbridge.org/high-school-students/national-college-match/who-should-apply

View more Frequently Asked Questions (FAQs) and more information on the QuestBridge Collegematch Scholarship application website.

☑ **Application Link: https://www.questbridge.org/high-school-students**

21. THE COOKE COLLEGE SCHOLARSHIP PROGRAM

JACK KENT COOKE FOUNDATION
COLLEGE SCHOLARSHIP

OVERVIEW

The Cooke College Scholarship program is awarded annually, it covers a student's tuition, living expenses, books and required fees throughout years of undergraduate study.

Also, recipients have access to one-on-one advising about selecting a college, navigating financial aid, transitioning to college, and maximizing the college experience; And may be eligible to apply for the **Cooke Graduate Scholarship**.

It is available to high-achieving high school seniors with financial need who seek to attend and graduate from the nation's best four-year colleges and universities. Scholars are allowed to study a field of their choice.

The Jack Kent Cooke Foundation is dedicated to advancing the education of exceptionally promising students who have financial need. Since 2000, the Foundation has awarded over $230 million in scholarships to more than 2,930 students from 8th grade through graduate school, along with comprehensive educational advising and other support services. The Foundation has also provided $119.5 million in grants to organizations that serve such students.

Who was Jack Kent Cooke?
Mr. Cooke was a philanthropist, businessman, and devotee of learning and the arts who left the bulk of his estate to establish the Jack Kent Cooke Foundation to help students of exceptional promise reach their full potential through education.

The deadline for this scholarship is usually around October 30th Annually

FULL RIDE EXTERNAL SCHOLARSHIPS

Frequently Asked Questions

Do I have to attend college in the U.S.?
No, you do not have to attend college in the U.S., but you must attend a fully accredited four-year institution to pursue a baccalaureate degree.

Must I be a U.S. citizen to apply?
No. You must, however, reside in the United States or a U.S. territory and attend high school in the United States. At this time, the Jack Kent Cooke Foundation is not providing services to students who attend high school outside of the United States.

Are there restrictions on fields of study for Cooke College Scholarship recipients?
You can pursue a baccalaureate degree in the field of study of your choice. However, non-degree programs are not eligible.

If I am home schooled, am I eligible to apply?
Yes, homeschooled students are eligible to apply.

You are strongly encouraged to request your two recommendations from educators other than your parents, for example, a professor from any dual-enrollment college courses, someone who has mentored you in a tutorial, the local librarian with whom you've discussed books over the years, or someone in whose lab you have done research.

Selection Criteria

Cooke College Scholarship recipients are selected from a nationwide applicant pool each year. As minimum criteria, students must:

- Plan to graduate from a U.S. high school in spring of application year.
- Intend to enroll full time in an accredited 4- year college in fall of application year.
- Earn a cumulative unweighted GPA of 3.5 or above in high school.
- Demonstrate financial need. It considers applicants with family income up to $95,000. Last year's cohort of new College Scholarship recipients had a median family income of approximately $35,000

Cooke Scholars come from diverse racial and ethnic backgrounds and from rural, suburban, and urban communities. Many Scholars are the first in their families to pursue higher education.

What if my parent(s)/guardian(s) or I do not file federal taxes?

If you or your parents do not file federal taxes, you are required to provide estimated financial information. You must also include an explanation regarding your family's financial circumstances.

View more Frequently Asked Questions (FAQs) and more information on the Cooke Scholarship Program Site.

☑ **Application Link:**
https://www.jkcf.org/our-scholarships/college-scholarship-program/

22 THE FLINN FOUNDATION SCHOLARSHIP

OVERVIEW

The Flinn Foundation Scholarship is awarded annually, it covers a student's tuition, fees, housing, and meals throughout the student's undergraduate years of study.

Applicants must study at one of Arizona's three public universities, and the scholarship includes a study abroad package as well.

The student must be a U.S. citizen or lawful permanent resident(Green Card holder) by the time of application. Also, student(s) must be an Arizona resident.

As a general rule, Flinn Scholarship applicants should also:
- Attain at least a 3.5 grade-point average (unweighted);
- Rank in the top 5 percent of their graduating class (if the school reports class rank); and
- Participate and demonstrate leadership in a variety of extracurricular activities.

The Flinn Foundation is a privately endowed, philanthropic grant-making organization established in 1965 by Dr. Robert S. and Irene P. Flinn.

It's mission is to improve the quality of life in Arizona to benefit future generations.
To achieve this mission, the Foundation aims to advance the state's bioscience sector, provide a top-notch education to high-achieving students at an Arizona public university, boost the fiscal and creative capacity of the state's arts and culture organizations, and develop future state-level civic leaders.

The deadline for this scholarship is usually around Mid-september annually.

FULL RIDE EXTERNAL SCHOLARSHIPS

Frequently Asked Questions

Can home-schooled students apply for the Flinn Scholarship?

Yes. The counselor recommendation and transcript are typically provided by the parent who took primary responsibility for the student's education. That recommendation must provide information about the curriculum and home-schooling approach. The other two recommendations must be from persons who taught the student at an accredited institution: high school, community college, or university. The Foundation would receive independent assessment of the student's academic and social performance in a group context.

What if I'm not in the top 5% of my class but I have a 4.0 or close to it? Can I still apply?

Many students from small or college-prep schools may not be in the top 5% of their classes, despite high academic achievement. We still encourage you to apply.

Does it matter what I list as my potential major or career interests?

No. Scholars can choose to major in any field of study/career of their choice.

Flinn Scholarship Application Requirement

To be awarded the Flinn Scholarship, an applicant must:
- Be a U.S. citizen or lawful permanent resident (Green Card holder) by time of application;
- Be an Arizona resident for two full years immediately preceding entry to the university.

As a general rule, Flinn Scholarship applicants should also:
- Attain at least a 3.5 grade-point average (unweighted);
- Rank in the top 5 percent of their graduating class (if the school reports class rank); and
- Participate and demonstrate leadership in a variety of extracurricular activities.

What does the Flinn Scholars Program expect of Flinn Scholars?

Scholars submit an annual narrative about their coursework, on- and off-campus activities, career plans, and overall college experience. They must maintain a 3.2 cumulative grade-point average and participate in at least two Foundation-related activities each academic year.

View more Frequently Asked Questions (FAQs) and more information on the Flinn Scholarship Site.

☑ **Application Link: https://flinn.org/flinn-scholars/**

DOD SMART SCHOLARSHIP

OVERVIEW

The **SMART** Program, part of the Department of Defense (DoD) science, technology, engineering and mathematics (STEM) portfolio, provides **STEM** students with the tools needed to pursue higher education and begin a rewarding career with the **DoD**.

SMART Scholars are provided with the tools required to pursue their **STEM** education and begin their career in a prestigious civilian position with the Department of Defense (DoD).
Benefits include:
- Full tuition and education related educational expenses (meal plans, housing, and parking not included)
- Stipend paid at a rate of $25,000 - $38,000 a year depending on degree level (may be prorated depending on award length)
- Summer research internships ranging from 8 to 12 weeks
- Health Insurance allowance of up to $1,200 per academic year
- Miscellaneous allowance of up to $1,000 per academic year
- An experienced mentor at one of the Sponsoring Facilities
- Employment placement at a DoD facility upon degree completion.

Scholarships are awarded for a minimum of 1 year and a maximum of 5 years of funding, depending on degree requirements. **SMART** is a one-for-one commitment; for every year of degree funding, the scholar commits to working for a year with the **DoD** as a civilian employee.

The deadline for this scholarship is usually around December 1st Annually.
It usually opens August 1st every year.

FULL RIDE EXTERNAL SCHOLARSHIPS

Frequently Asked Questions

What kind of STEM?

The program focuses on students pursuing disciplines that are critical to national security functions of the Department of Defense (DoD). The following is a list of SMART's 21 approved STEM disciplines. These disciplines are general umbrella disciplines – specific applicant majors or fields of study may fall under one or more discipline on this list.

Please note, non-technical degrees, including management, arts, or humanities, are not approved or funded by SMART.

- Aeronautical and Astronautical Engineering
- Biosciences
- Biomedical Engineering
- Chemical Engineering
- Chemistry
- Civil Engineering
- Cognitive, Neural, and Behavioral Sciences
- Computer and Computational Sciences and Computer Engineering
- Electrical Engineering
- Environmental Sciences
- Geosciences
- Industrial and Systems Engineering
- Information Sciences
- Materials Science and Engineering
- Mathematics
- Mechanical Engineering
- Naval Architecture and Ocean Engineering
- Nuclear Engineering
- Oceanography
- Operations Research
- Physics

Eligibility Requirements

Who can apply?

The SMART application is open August through December of every year, with awards being granted the following spring. Review the below requirements to ensure you are eligible to apply for this life-changing opportunity. All applicants must be:

- a citizen of the United States, Australia, Canada, New Zealand, or United Kingdom at time of application,
- 18 years of age or older as of August 1, 2023
- requesting at least 1 year of degree funding prior to graduation (which starts at the program start date),
- able to complete at least one summer internship (multi-year scholars only)
- willing to accept post-graduation employment with the DoD,
- a student in good standing with a minimum cumulative GPA of 3.0 on a 4.0 scale,
- pursuing a technical undergraduate or graduate degree in one of the 21 STEM disciplines listed below,
- able to produce a fall 2022 college transcript from a regionally accredited US college or university, OR be pursuing a graduate degree at a regionally accredited US college or university.

Active duty military members who wish to apply for the SMART Scholarship must be separated or on terminal leave on or before August 1, 2023 to be eligible. Reserve and National Guard members are eligible to apply. Current ROTC participants with a future service commitment are not eligible to apply

FULL RIDE EXTERNAL SCHOLARSHIPS

Frequently Asked Questions

Commitment Info:
Scholarships are awarded for a minimum of 1 year and a maximum of 5 years of funding, depending on degree requirements. SMART is a one-for-one commitment; for every year of degree funding, the scholar commits to working for a year with the DoD as a civilian employee.

Undergraduate Applicants
- Must be currently enrolled at a regionally accredited U.S. college or university
- Must be able to produce a fall 2022 (or earlier) college transcript at the end of the term
- AP coursework is not considered college credit

Can my award be deferred?

SMART scholarships generally may not be deferred. SMART Scholars begin or resume academic work in the term immediately following receipt of initial SMART funding.

How can I apply for a SMART Scholarship?

Applications are open from August 1 through December 1 every year. The application will be available online during this timeframe.

Review full application instructions here: https://www.smartscholarship.org/smart?id=kb_article&sys_id=0383c5d6db2a03006bb8f4b40f961956

When will I be notified if I received an award?
Semi-finalists are notified in early spring and award recipients are notified in the late spring (typically in April).

How is tuition paid?

Tuition and related educational fees will be paid directly to your university by Scholarship America. Upon acceptance of the award, scholars are provided with a sponsor letter to send to their university bursar's office with information about tuition payments and invoicing.

View more Frequently Asked Questions (FAQs) and more information on the DoD SMART Scholarship website.

☑ **Application Link: https://www.smartscholarship.org/smart**

24. THE SCIENCE AMBASSADOR SCHOLARSHIP

OVERVIEW

The science ambassador scholarship is a full tuition scholarship for a woman in science, technology, engineering, or math. Funded by Cards Against Humanity.

This scholarship is for only female scholars.

It may be used at any accredited college or university in the United States.

The scholarship is open to only undergraduate and high school seniors.

Runner-ups will be awarded between $5,000 to $1,000 towards their tuition cost.

Frequently Asked Questions

Do I have to be a U.S. Citizen to apply?

You do not need to be a U.S. citizen to apply. You do need to attend college (or plan to attend college) in the United States or a United States Territory.

I haven't decided on a major, but I'm definitely going to study a STEM field. Can I still apply?

Yes, you can apply, as long as you will study a STEM field for the entirety of your undergraduate career.

How many years of tuition does this scholarship cover?

The scholarship pays the winner's undergraduate tuition expenses for up to four years. Please note that they do not reimburse the winner for tuition expenses incurred prior to winning this scholarship.

Can I apply if I'm a graduate student?

No. The Science Ambassador Scholarship is only open to undergraduate students and high school seniors.

Which fields of study are eligible?

All fields within science, technology, engineering, and math are eligible. For a full list of STEM fields, visit --- https://www.scienceambassadorscholarship.org/stem/
P.S: STEM must be your major field of study (not your minor).

View more Frequently Asked Questions (FAQs) and more information on the Science Ambassador Scholarship Website.

☑ **Application Link:** https://www.scienceambassadorscholarship.org/

THE 5 STRONG SCHOLARSHIP

OVERVIEW

5 Strong partners with Historically Black Colleges and Universities (HBCUs) to provide promising student leaders with full-tuition scholarships and ongoing mentorship and support from matriculation to graduation.

The scholarship may only be used only at a 5-Strong HBCU partner College(s)/Universities.

For years, as a teacher and counselor, 5 Strong founder Andrew Ragland watched HBCUs (Historically Black Colleges and Universities) nurture his former students, especially the ones without outstanding scores but plenty of potential. An HBCU graduate himself, Ragland and his team believe these institutions are uniquely positioned to give students who might be overlooked the support they need to shine.

In 2015, Ragland opened 5 Strong, and began linking students waiting to shine with **HBCUs** that he knew can best help them on their journey to become change makers and leaders. 5 Strong worked with **HBCUs** to arrange full-tuition scholarships so a lack of money wouldn't stand in the way of young scholars' dreams; And Ragland built an intensive college success program run by an experienced team ready to embrace their students like family. Today, this model has been proven: more and more **HBCUs** are signing on, and 84% of 5 Strong's scholars are on track to graduate — more than twice the national average.

The deadline for this scholarship is usually around December 31st Annually.

FULL RIDE EXTERNAL SCHOLARSHIPS

Frequently Asked Questions

When does the 5Strong Application Open?

The 5-strong scholarship application opens around August 15th each year. The deadline is by December 1st.

What Does the 5Strong Scholarship Cover?

The 5Strong Scholarship is a very generous college scholarships. It covers a student's full tuition for all the years of undergraduate studies.

How old is the 5Strong Scholarship Program?

The 5strong Scholars Program was launched in the year 2015.

Do I need to Submit an SAT/ACT Score?

Most of the HBCU partners still require that 5 Strong applicants submit standardized test scores (ACT/SAT) in order to receive the full tuition scholarships. All applicants must still take either the ACT or SAT before submitting an application or your application will be deleted.

Must students come from a particular area?

Yes, student must come from the Houston or Atlanta areas(or surrounding areas) of the United States of America.

Can I utilize the 5strong scholarship at any University of choice?

No, the scholarship must be utilized at a 5strong partner HBCU university/college.

View more Frequently Asked Questions (FAQs) and more information on the 5strong Scholarship Site.

☑ **Application Link: https://www.5strongscholars.org/apply**

26. THE ROBERTSON SCHOLARS PROGRAM

OVERVIEW

The Robertson Scholars Leadership Program provides eight semesters of full tuition, room and board, and most mandatory fees for Scholars at Duke and UNC-Chapel Hill. Scholars also have access to generous funding for up to three summer experiences, funding for conferences throughout the academic year, and for two semesters of study abroad.

It may be used either at Duke University or University of North Carolina, Chapel Hill.

Julian H. Robertson, Jr. and his late wife, Josie, are the founders of the Robertson Scholars Leadership Program. In 2000, the Robertson family donated $24 million to create The Robertson Scholars Leadership Program in his native North Carolina, to encourage collaboration between Duke and the University of North Carolina and to promote the development of young leaders.

The first class of Robertson Scholars graduated in 2005. Robertson Scholars continue to make impacts on both campuses and within the Chapel Hill and Durham communities, much like Julian and Josie had envisioned. Collaborations between Duke and UNC Scholars have resulted in start-ups, non-profits, research collaborations, and more.

Mr. Robertson and his sons continue to work alongside the Robertson Program staff to make this a one-of-a-kind Program.

The deadline for this scholarship is usually around January 26th Annually.

FULL RIDE EXTERNAL SCHOLARSHIPS

Frequently Asked Questions

Is any particular major required for Robertson Scholars?

Robertson Scholars may major in any subject offered at their home institution. Scholars may also double major, minor, or obtain a certificate in a variety of subjects.

What is expected of Robertson Scholars?

Robertson Scholars participate in mandatory programs, including but not limited to: retreats, the campus switch, cross-campus coursework, community events, and at least two summer enrichment programs (domestic and international, following the Scholar's first and second years, respectively). The Robertson Scholars Leadership Program expects all Scholars to uphold the academic standards for which they were awarded the scholarship.

How old is the Robertson Scholars Program?

The Coolidge Scholars Program launched in the 2000 and the inaugural class was formally inducted in July 2005.

Do I need to submit an official transcript for my Robertson Program application?

No. However, you will need to be able to provide certain details from your transcript in the application (e.g., GPA, SAT/ACT, AP/IB scores). In addition, you must submit an official transcript as part of your university admissions application to Duke and/or UNC.

Who can Apply for the Robertson?

Both U.S. and international student are eligible to apply for the Robertson scholars program.

Are Robertson Scholars Duke or UNC-Chapel Hill Students?

While all Robertson Scholars have full student privileges at both universities, each Scholar matriculates at and graduates from only one of the two universities. However, each Scholar will take a minimum of 5 courses at the sister university over the course of four years and Scholars' transcripts will reflect all cross-campus coursework and participation in the Robertson Scholars Leadership Program.

View more Frequently Asked Questions (FAQs) and more information on the Robertson Scholarship website.

☑ **Application Link: https://robertsonscholars.org/**

AIR FORCE ROTC (AFROTC) SCHOLARSHIP

OVERVIEW

The **US Airforce ROTC** scholarship is awarded annually, it covers the scholar's tuition, fees, and monthly living expense and annual book stipend.

It may be used at any of the **AFROTC** featured 1,100 colleges and universities in the continental United States, Puerto Rico and Hawaii.

The **US Airforce ROTC** are dedicated to developing leaders of tomorrow who will go on to fulfill the Air Force mission, represent the core values and live up to the rich history of Air Force ROTC.

This program promises more than just education. It offers:

- **Leadership opportunities**
- **Professional Development**
- **Start as a Manager (Enter the Air Force or Space Force an an officer and leader)**
- **Salary & Benefits.**

The deadline for this scholarship is usually around December 31th Annually.

FULL RIDE EXTERNAL SCHOLARSHIPS

Frequently Asked Questions

Where can the AFROTC be used?

Air Force ROTC is offered at over 1,100 colleges and universities in the continental United States, Puerto Rico and Hawaii. If you are applying for a scholarship as a high school student, you must be accepted to the program and academic major that you indicate on your scholarship application.

What majors are acceptable by the AFROTC?

Virtually all majors are accepted for the AFROTC program, but some are given a high priority. View the list of majors which are given a high priority here: https://www.afrotc.com/scholarships/desired-majors/

Must I be a high school student to apply for this scholarship?

The AFROTC has a program specific to high school students and another specific to already enrolled in College. However, the type specific to high school students have bigger benefits.

Selection Criteria

The AFROTC scholarship program have specific requirement which are categorized as follows:

- Academic Standards
- Fitness Requirements
- Medical Requirements
- Enlisted Requirements

The requirements can be viewed in details here:

https://www.afrotc.com/what-it-takes/

Are there specialised training that AFROTC scholars receive?

Yes, they receive AFROTC courses like specialized classes and hands-on leadership workshops.

View more Frequently Asked Questions (FAQs) and more information on the AFROTC Scholarship website.

☑ **Application Link: https://www.afrotc.com/scholarships/**

ARMY ROTC SCHOLARSHIP

OVERVIEW

The **US Army ROTC** is awarded annually, it can cover the scholar's tuition and fees, or room and board, and each comes with stipends for living and books.

Receive monthly stipends to offset costs of living and books.
- All scholarships include an extra $420 per month for the school year to use toward monthly expenses, like housing,
- All scholarships also allow $1,200 per year to spend toward books.

Your achievements and grades determine if you'll be awarded a scholarship, not your financial need.

It may be used at any of the Army ROTC featured 1,000 colleges and universities in the continental United States, Puerto Rico and Hawaii.

ARMY ROTC allows you become a leader and serve your country, all without sacrificing your college experience. In Army Reserve Officers' Training Corps (ROTC), a career is waiting for you when you graduate.
This program promises more than just education. It offers:

- Leadership opportunities
- Professional Development
- Start as a Manager (Enter the U.S. ARMY as an officer and leader)
- Salary & Benefits

The deadline for this scholarship is usually around February 4th Annually.

FULL RIDE EXTERNAL SCHOLARSHIPS

Frequently Asked Questions

If I enroll in Army ROTC, what is the service commitment?

Enrolling in the ROTC Basic Course (the first two years of college) does not obligate you to serve unless you receive a scholarship. If you received a four-year ROTC scholarship, you must agree to serve four years full-time as an Army Officer after you graduate and then either extend your contract for four more years or serve four more years with the Individual Ready Reserve (IRR) where you'll return to civilian life but need to be ready to help in a national emergency. If you received a three-year or two-year ROTC scholarship, you must agree to serve four years full-time as Army Officer after you graduate.

Can I still choose my major?

You may choose any major you wish and commission as an Officer into the active-duty Army, Army Reserve, or Army National Guard.

Must I be a high school student to apply for this scholarship?

You're eligible to apply for ROTC scholarship which could get you up to 100% tuition coverage if you're a high school student enrolling in college, currently-enrolled college student, or an active enlisted Soldier.

Standard Requirements for ROTC Scholarships

To be accepted for any ROTC Scholarship, you must meet these standards:

- Be a U.S. citizen
- Be at least 17, and under 31 in year of commissioning
- Have a high school diploma or equivalent
- Have a high school GPA of at least 2.50, unweighted if you're in high school while applying
- Have taken the SAT or ACT
- Pass the current Army physical fitness test
- Meet the physical weight and height requirements -- https://www.goarmy.com/learn/army-requirements-and-qualifications.html#height
- Agree to accept a commission and serve in the Army on Active Duty or in Army Reserve or Army National Guard

What are Army ROTC courses like?

In college, Army ROTC classes normally involve one elective class and one lab per semester. Although the classes involve hands-on fieldwork as well as classroom work, they are standard college classes that fit into a normal academic schedule.

View more Frequently Asked Questions (FAQs) and more information on the Army ROTC Scholarship website.

☑ **Application Link:**

https://www.goarmy.com/careers-and-jobs/find-your-path/army-officers/rotc/scholarships.html

THE MINUTEMAN CAMPAIGN UNDER THE ARMY ROTC SCHOLARSHIP

OVERVIEW

The Minuteman is a Guaranteed Reserve Forces Duty (GRFD) scholarship that provides full in-state tuition and fees, or up to $10,000 room and board between 2-4 years for eligible candidates. The Minuteman scholarship guarantees the candidate will commission into the USAR upon graduation with an eight-year service obligation.

If you are a high school senior interested in receiving an Army Reserve Officer Training Corps (ROTC) scholarship and commissioning into the Army Reserve, the GRFD Scholarship Minuteman Campaign provides you an excellent opportunity.

The Minuteman campaign offers two types of 4 year scholarships.
1) 4-year scholarship may only be awarded to incoming college freshmen attending a host ROTC program or a public university at resident rates.
2) 3-year awarded to an incoming college sophomore that pays the last 3 years of benefits provided the applicant successfully meets the requirements to contract.
3) 2-year awarded to an incoming college junior or graduate student that pays the last 2 years of benefits provided the applicant successfully meets the requirements to contract.

FULL RIDE EXTERNAL SCHOLARSHIPS

Scholarship recipients also receive a monthly stipend of $420, and a yearly book allowance of $1,200. In addition, Minuteman recipients participate in the Simultaneous Membership Program, which gives them experience with an Army Reserve unit while earning additional money for their service.

To get started, high school seniors should contact the Professor of Military Science or Recruiting Operations Officer at the Army ROTC program that serves their college or university. There are 275 host programs that cover nearly 3,000 schools across the United States.

SCHOLARSHIP BENEFITS:
- Receive full tuition and fees (in-state) or room and board ($10,000 per year) at the participating University of attendance
- Receive Cadet stipend monthly ($420 Freshman-Senior)
- Receive a book stipend of $1,200 annually ($600 per semester)

REQUIREMENTS:
- Minimum high school GPA: 2.5
- Minimum test scores: SAT 850 or ACT 19
- Enlisted or Eligible to enlist
- Must be a U.S. Citizen
- Eligible to participate in the Simultaneous Membership Program(SMP), an experience with an Army Reserve unit while earning additional money for service
- Meet physical fitness requirements
- Between the age(s) of 17-28

Application deadline is usually around August 5th Yearly.

View more information about the Minuteman Campaign on their website below:

☑ **Application Link:**
https://www.usar.army.mil/MinutemanCampaign/

NAVAL ROTC SCHOLARSHIP

OVERVIEW

The **US Navy ROTC** is awarded annually, it can cover the scholar's tuition and fees, three(3) summer cruises, stipends for living and books.

Subsistence allowance each academic month: Freshmen - $250/month | Sophomore - $300/month | Junior - $350/month | Senior - $400/month.

The purpose of the **Navy ROTC Program** is to educate and train qualified young men and women for service as commissioned officers in the **Navy's** unrestricted line, the **Navy Nurse Corps and the Marine Corps.** As the largest single source of **Navy and Marine Corps** officers, the **Navy ROTC Scholarship Program** plays an important role in preparing mature young men and women for leadership and management positions in an increasingly technical **Navy and Marine Corps.**

Students may start the process of applying during the second semester of their junior year of high school. Students may apply for only one of the three scholarship program options-Navy, Nurse or Marine Corps.

The Naval Reserve Officers Training Corps (Navy ROTC) Program was established in 1926 to provide a broad base of citizens knowledgeable in the arts and sciences of Naval Warfare. The program provided an opportunity for young men to undertake careers in the naval profession. In the beginning, there were six **Navy ROTC** units located at the University of California at Berkeley, Georgia Institute of Technology, Northwestern University, University of Washington, and Harvard and Yale Universities. In June of 1930, 126 midshipmen graduated from college, and received commissions in the United States Navy. At least 3 of the graduates went on to obtain flag rank.

The deadline for this scholarship is usually around Februar 4th Annually.

FULL RIDE EXTERNAL SCHOLARSHIPS

Frequently Asked Questions

What programs are available?
Navy Option

Marine Corps Option

Navy Nurse Corps Option

Selection Criteria
View the detailed selection criteria for the NROTC program here: https://www.netc.navy.mil/Commands/Naval-Service-Training-Command/NROTC/Requirements/

What is expected of me in Navy ROTC?

Navy ROTC midshipmen are required to complete the course of study prescribed by the college or university that they attend. Midshipmen are also required to take several naval science courses in addition to their college's prescribes course load. Due to the increasing complexity of today's Navy, Navy option midshipmen are required to complete the equivalent of two semesters of calculus before the end of their sophomore year and two semesters of calculus based physics before the end of their junior year.

What do I owe the Navy or Marine Corps after graduation?
View the full terms here: https://www.netc.navy.mil/Commands/Naval-Service-Training-Command/NROTC/Requirements/

What happens after graduation?

Upon graduation, midshipmen who complete all academic requirements in the Navy ROTC program are commissioned as Ensigns in the Navy or Second Lieutenants in the Marine Corps. Although it is not current policy, in the future some midshipmen may be commissioned temporarily into the Individual Ready Reserve (IRR). Midshipmen without scholarships may also receive a commission through the College Program.

View more Frequently Asked Questions (FAQs) and more information on the NROTC website.

☑ **Application Link: https://www.netc.navy.mil/NSTC/NROTC/**

31. Onsi Sawiris Scholarship Program

ONSI SAWIRIS
SCHOLARSHIP PROGRAM

OVERVIEW

The Onsi Sawiris Scholarship Program is a fully funded scholarship program for undergraduate and graduate students. The scholarship is open for all Egyptian students seeking to pursue their degrees at prestigious universities in the United States with the aim of bolstering Egypt's economic competitiveness.

This program is a precedent in Egypt for private sector involvement in educational programs on a sustainable basis. The aim of which is to facilitate the academic development and character building of young Egyptians giving them the tools to develop their careers hence benefiting their communities in which they live.

The Onsi Sawiris Scholarship Program is only granted to the list of endorsed universities provided in the "Approved Universities" Selection as a nominee for the Onsi Sawiris scholarship Program does not guarantee university acceptance. Applicants will be supported in applying to these universities. If nominated for the scholarship; the Onsi Sawiris Scholarship Program award will be made once university acceptance is obtained.

List of Approved Universities:
- Stanford University
- Harvard University
- University of Chicago
- University of Pennsylvania.

The deadline for this scholarship is July 31st.

FULL RIDE EXTERNAL SCHOLARSHIPS

Frequently Asked Questions

When does the Onsi Sawiris Scholarship Program Application Open?

Applicants should download and submit an application form documents required before July 31st.

What does the Onsi Sawiris Scholarship Program Cover?

The Onsi Sawiris Scholarships are awarded based on merit, need and character as demonstrated through academic excellence, extracurricular activities, and entrepreneurial initiative. The scholarships include full tuition, living allowance, travel expenses, health insurance and other benefits.

I'm an international student, am I eligible to apply for the Onsi Sawiris Scholarship Program?

Applicants must be Egyptian nationals, who are residents of Egypt (preference will **not** be given to holders of dual nationality).

Selection Criteria

Applicants should have a minimum GPA of 3.5/90% in Thanaweyya Amma certification (Secondary year) or equivalent certificates.

TOEFL iBT ®: 100 or above (taken within 2 years).

Minimum SAT I Score: 1450 (Taken within 2 years) or Minimum ACT Score: 32 (Taken within 2 years)

Extracurricular Activities: Have been involved or are currently involved in extracurricular activities.

Fields of Study: Engineering, Economics, Political Science, Finance and Management.

Be Egyptian nationals, who are residents of Egypt (preference will not be given to dual nationality applicants).

Be committed to coming back to Egypt for two years directly after the successful completion of their bachelor's degree.

P.S: Preference will be given to candidates who have not lived, worked, or studied abroad for a significant period of time.

How old is the Onsi Sawiris Scholarship Program?

The Onsi Sawiris Scholarship is a private merit-based scholarship program established in 2000 by Orascom Construction as part of the company's commitment to promoting excellence and achievement.

View more details and more information on the Onsi Sawiris Scholarship Program website.

☑ **Application Link: https://www.onsisawirisscholarship.org/**

CHAPTER 3

FULL RIDE NEED-BASED $CHOLARSHIP$

Princeton University

Location: Princeton, New Jersey
Setting: Suburban (600 Acres)
Undergraduate Enrollment: 4,773
Type: Private
Acceptance Rate: 6%
Early Acceptance Rate: 14.7%

Financial aid Admission at Princeton university is awarded solely based on financial need, there are no merit scholarship awards. Princeton's admissions is need-blind for all applicants, including international students.

The student's need is determined through a careful review of each family's individual financial circumstances. Most importantly, the full need of every admitted student is met through grants.

Application Deadline: Usually around November 9th

Application link: https://admission.princeton.edu/cost-aid/apply-financial-aid

View more information using the table below:

Gross Family Income	Percent Qualified	Average Grant	What It Covers
$0 – 65,000	100%	$77,240	Full tuition, room + board
$65,000 – 85,000	100%	$70,520	Full tuition, 80% room + board
$85,000 – 100,000	100%	$68,180	Full tuition, 67% room + board
$100,000 – 120,000	100%	$65,750	Full tuition, 54% room + board
$120,000 – 140,000	100%	$62,780	Full tuition, 37% room + board

Continued on Next Page >>>

Join Our Mailing List Here: https://bit.ly/chrisnuel-publishing

IVY LEAGUE & TOP COLLEGES

Gross Family Income	Percent Qualified	Average Grant	What It Covers
$140,000 – 160,000	100%	$57,550	Full tuition, 8% room + board
$160,000 – 180,000	100%	$53,360	95% tuition
$180,000 – 200,000	98%	$44,440	79% tuition
$200,000 – 250,000	95%	$68,180	66% tuition
$250,000 and above (most who qualify have 2 children in college	43%	$68,180	51% tuition

Full tuition = $68,180

Room and board = $18,180

For detailed information about the Princeton scholarship and how to apply for the need based scholarship – Use the link below:

Application link: https://admission.princeton.edu/cost-aid/apply-financial-aid

Harvard University

Location: Cambridge, Massachusetts
Setting: Urban (5,076 Acres)
Undergraduate Enrollment: 5,222
Type: Private
Acceptance Rate: 5%
Early Acceptance Rate: 13.9%

" 55%" of students receive need-based Harvard scholarships. 1 in 5 pays nothing to attend."

Harvard scholarships are orchestrated to cover 100% of a student's demonstrated financial need.

Below is Harvard's Aid Process:

- First they determine your award by establishing your parent contribution (https://college.harvard.edu/financial-aid/how-aid-works#determining-need).
- Then they factor in student employment and any outside awards the student has received.
- Your remaining need will be covered by scholarship funds which are grant-based and never need to be repaid.

US Citizens, permanent residents and international students are eligible for Harvard need-based scholarships.

US Citizens and Permanent Residents

US citizens and permanent residents may be eligible to receive a Federal Pell Grant or a Supplemental Educational Opportunity Grant (SEOG). The scholar's eligibility is determined by the information they provide in their Free Application for Federal Student Aid (FAFSA).

Pell Grants and SEOG are awarded by the federal government and administered by Harvard's office, based on financial need. Roughly 17% of Harvard College students are Pell Grant recipients.

Application Link: https://college.harvard.edu/financial-aid/how-aid-works/types-aid

Yale University

Location: New Haven, Connecticut
Setting: City (373 Acres)
Undergraduate Enrollment: 4,703
Type: Private
Acceptance Rate: 7%

A **Yale financial aid** award meets 100% of a student's demonstrated financial need based on the estimated cost of attendance and a calculated expected family contribution. This is done regardless of citizenship or immigration status—without relying on student loans, for all four years.

Every Yale financial aid award includes two parts: grant aid and the Student Share. Grant aid may include a need-based Yale Scholarship and/or funds from external sources including entitlement grants (Federal Pell Grant, Supplemental Educational Opportunity Grant/SEOG, and state grants) or merit-based scholarships a student may have earned from outside organizations. Yale does not give out any merit-based scholarships.

The Student Share is a fixed amount students receiving aid should anticipate contributing from term-time and summer job earnings. The grant aid and Student Effort in every Yale financial aid award will meet a student's full demonstrated financial need.

Application Link:

https://finaid.yale.edu/costs-affordability/affordability

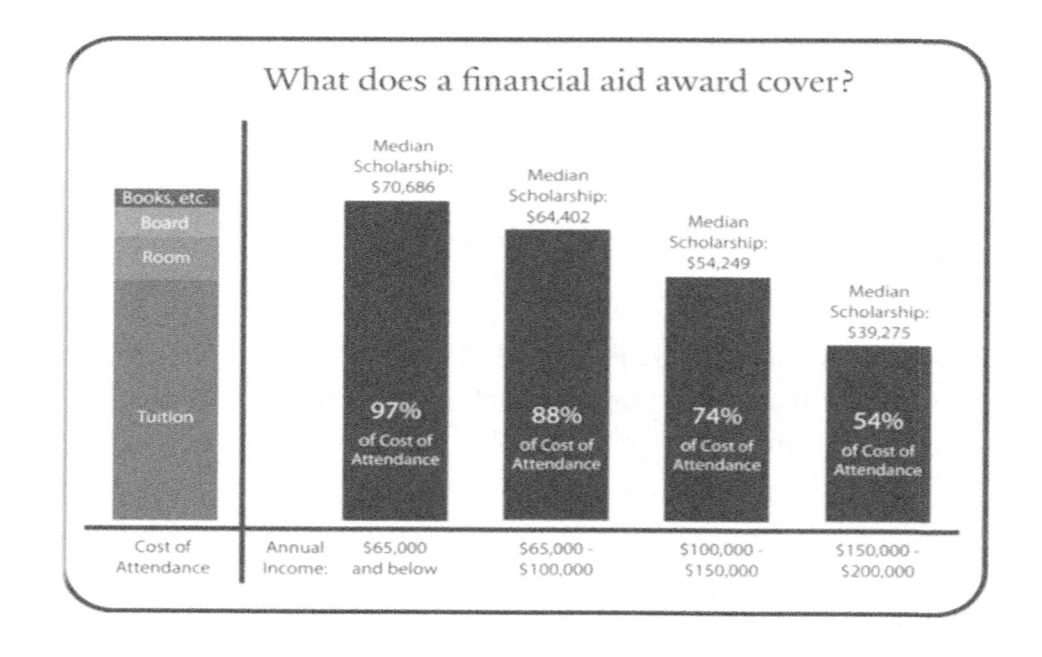

What does a financial aid award cover?

Annual Income	Median Scholarship	% of Cost of Attendance
$65,000 and below	$70,686	97%
$65,000 – $100,000	$64,402	88%
$100,000 – $150,000	$54,249	74%
$150,000 – $200,000	$39,275	54%

Cost of Attendance: Tuition, Room, Board, Books, etc.

Columbia University

Location: New York, New York
Setting: Urban (36 Acres)
Undergraduate Enrollment: 6,170
Type: Private
Acceptance Rate: 5%
Early Acceptance Rate: 13.9%

Scholarships/Financial aid at Columbia University is totally need based. They evaluate the student's family ability to pay for education costs. In Columbia, there are no academic, athletic or talent-based institutional scholarships.

Columbia evaluates admission applications of US Citizens and Eligible Non-Citizens without regard to your financial need. Admissions for international students are however need aware.

At Columbia University, 100% of the demonstrated financial need for all first-years and transfers pursuing their first degree are met. Up to all four years of study. International students are also highly considered.

About Columbia University Financial Aid Programs:

- No loans – Columbia's need-based aid is in the form of grants and student work only. Loans are not used to meet financial need or included in initial financial aid awards.
- $0 parent contribution - For students coming from families with calculated total incomes of less than $66,000 annually (and typical assets), parents are not expected to contribute to the cost of attendance.
- Free Tuition - Students coming from families with calculated total incomes of less than $150,000 annually (and typical assets) will be able to attend Columbia tuition-free.
- Start-Up Grants
- Broad Aid Eligibility
- Funding Opportunities
- International Aid
- Guidance for All

Application Link: https://cc-seas.financialaid.columbia.edu/how/aid/works

5 Brown University

Location: Providence, Rhode Island
Setting: City (146 Acres)
Undergraduate Enrollment: 6,792
Type: Private
Acceptance Rate: 8%

The Sidney E. Frank Scholarship is awarded to the neediest undergraduate students at Brown University who cannot otherwise afford the full cost of tuition and other costs of receiving an education at Brown.

In September 2004, Sidney E. Frank, a member of the class of 1942, made a gift of $100 million to Brown University — the largest gift in the University's history.

Eligibity & Selection Criteria

Undergraduate students who are U.S. citizens or eligible non-citizens and who enter Brown through the Early Admission and Regular Admission process will be eligible for consideration as Frank Scholars.

There is no separate application required. Students who meet the criteria will automatically be considered assuming that all financial aid application requirements and deadlines are met.

For More Information visit the Sidney E. Frank Scholarship page and/or send an email to the financial aid office:

Application Link: https://finaid.brown.edu/aid-types/grants-scholarships/sidney-e-frank-scholars

6. Dartmouth College

Location: Hanover, New Hampshire
Setting: Rural (237 Acres)
Undergraduate Enrollment: 4,170
Type: Private
Acceptance Rate: 9%

Dartmouth Scholarships and endowment grants are need-based and are given without expectation of repayment. Amounts range from $1,000 to over $50,000, depending on our determination of your eligibility

Dartmouth can cover 100% of student's cost of attendance based on the student's need.

Cost of Education − Family Contribution = "Need"

There is zero parent contribution for families with income below $65,000

Dartmouth's Tuition Guarantee
Students from families with total incomes of $125,000 or less—and possessing typical assets, will receive scholarship that will at least cover the cost of tuition.

Families with Income Above $125,000
There is no income cut off for scholarship consideration at Dartmouth. We take an individual look at all applications, and families earning over $125,000 per year do receive scholarship assistance.

Application Link: https://financialaid.dartmouth.edu/apply-aid/prospective-transfer-Linstudents/how-apply-aid

IMPORTANT DEADLINES

Early Decision
CSS Profile: November 1
FAFSA: November 1
IDOC: November 1

Regular Decision
CSS Profile: February 1
FAFSA: February 1
IDOC: February 1

Transfer Students
CSS Profile: March 1
FAFSA: March 1
IDOC: March 1

Cornell University

Location: Ithaca, New York
Setting: Rural (745 Acres)
Undergraduate Enrollment: 14,743
Type: Private
Acceptance Rate: 11%

Cornell University Grant & Scholarships

Cornell Grants and scholarships are available to students with financial need, as determined by the Office of Financial Aid and Student Employment. The aid comes from several sources - university endowments, alumni gifts, and a general fund. Things to keep in mind:

There is no minimum or maximum amount of grant awarded.
There is no standard "income bracket" or cut-off for grant aid recipients; eligibility is determined on a case-by-case basis.
University grants are awarded after non-university funds, work-study, and loans.
You are automatically considered for these funds when you apply for financial aid; there is no separate application process.

Application Link: https://finaid.cornell.edu/types-aid

Massachusetts Institute of Technology

Location: Cambridge, Massachusetts
Setting: Urban (168 Acres)
Undergraduate Enrollment: 4,361
Type: Private
Acceptance Rate: 7%
Early Acceptance Rate: 7.4%

MIT is committed to meeting 100% of demonstrated financial need for both domestic students (U.S. citizens and Permanent residents) and international students.

About 60% of MIT undergraduates receive scholarships.

MIT Aid Application Deadlines.

Application deadlines are the same for both domestic and international students.
- Early Action applicants: November 30. The application deadline for Early Action is November 30 and awards are released in mid-January.
- Regular Action applicants: February 15. The application deadline is February 15, and awards are released in mid-March.
- Continuing students: April 15. The financial aid application deadline for the following academic year is April 15. You will receive your award in late May or early June.

Three Steps to Apply for Aid (For Domestic Students)
- FAFSA: the form you need to fill out to receive any federal or state student aid
- CSS Profile: a tool provided by the College Board that we use to determine if you qualify for a need-based MIT Scholarship
- Parental tax returns or income documentation: Your parents' tax returns or income documentation must be submitted through the College Board's secure IDOC platform.

Two Steps to Apply for Aid (For International Students)
- CSS Profile: A tool provided by the College Board that we use to determine if you qualify for a need-based MIT Scholarship.
- Parental tax returns or income documentation: your parents' tax returns or income documentation must be submitted through the College Board's secure IDOC platform. If your parents live outside the U.S., please provide the tax return from that country, along with a translation to English if applicable.

Application Link: https://sfs.mit.edu/undergraduate-students/types-of-aid/mit-scholarship/

Stanford University

Location: Stanford, California
Setting: Suburban (8,180 Acres)
Undergraduate Enrollment: 6,366
Type: Private
Acceptance Rate: 5%

Almost half of all Stanford undergraduates receive need-based financial aid. Families earning less than $150,000 with assets typical of that income level pay no tuition. Families earning less than $75,000 with assets typical of that income level pay no tuition or room and board.

The need based scholarships are available for both domestic (U.S. Citizens & permanent residents) and international students.

Total (Gross) Family Income	Average Scholarship and Grant	Average Net Cost	% of applicants who qualify for scholarship aid from Stanford
Less than $75,000	82,356	$4,118	99%
75,000 – 100,000	73,906	8,180	96%
100,000 – 125,000	66,256	14,404	100%
125,000 – 150,000	59.971	20,840	100%
150,000 – 175,000	51,210	29,558	94%
175,000 – 200,000	43,745	36,913	89%

Continued on Next Page >>>

IVY LEAGUE & TOP COLLEGES

Total (Gross) Family Income	Average Scholarship and Grant	Average Net Cost	% of applicants who qualify for scholarship aid from Stanford
200,000 – 225,000	35,663	44,956	93%
225,000 – 250,000	34,040	46.665	90%
250,000 – 275,000*	23,146	57,471	63%
$275,000 – 300,000*	21.768	58,897	56%
Greater than $300,000*	21,768	58,897	56%

*most who qualify have 2(or more) children in college.

Factors such as family size, number of family members in college and family asset are also considered.

Learn more here:
https://admission.stanford.edu/afford/

You can contact Stanford's admission office for more information.

California Institute of Technology

Location: Pasadena, California
Setting: Suburban (124 Acres)
Undergraduate Enrollment: 909
Type: Private
Acceptance Rate: 7%

Caltech will meet 100% of a student's demonstrated financial need through a combination of awards known as a financial aid package. These needs are met through grants, scholarships, and student employment.

Cost of Attendance − Family Contribution = Demonstrated Financial Need

Learn more about family contribution here:
https://www.finaid.caltech.edu/HowItWorks/familycontribution

The Cost of Attendance is the total cost of attending Caltech for one year. It includes both direct charges from Caltech, like tuition and fees, as well as other expenses, like books and supplies.

The Family Contribution represents the amount of money your family would be expected to pay for one year of school. They calculate the exact amount of your family's contribution with their needs analysis formula.

Caltech Financial Aid Scholarship: https://www.finaid.caltech.edu/Applying

Learn more about the Caltech Financial aid above or by contacting their admission office.

University of Chicago

11

Location: Chicago, Illinois
Setting: Urban (217 Acres)
Undergraduate Enrollment: 6,989
Type: Private
Acceptance Rate: 7%

UChicago meets 100% of demonstrated need in the form of grants (which do not need to be repaid) instead of loans for all families.

Cost of Attendance − Family Contribution = Demonstrated Financial Need

Your family contribution is then subtracted from the total cost of attendance. The cost of attendance represents actual and estimated costs for one year at UChicago, including tuition, housing, a meal plan, and estimates for additional costs like books and personal expenses.

Learn more about applying as a domestic candidate here:
https://collegeadmissions.uchicago.edu/financial-support/applying-aid

Learn more about applying as a international candidate here:
https://collegeadmissions.uchicago.edu/financial-support/applying-aid

CHAPTER 4

SCHOLARSHIP APPLICATION TIPS

SCHOLARSHIP APPLICATION GUIDELINES

Dear scholarship award aspirants, we have listed out the various full ride scholarships that are available for undergraduate study at universities and colleges in the United States. These scholarships are available to both U.S. residents and international students (unless otherwise indicated).

Instead of writing wordy sentences, we will go straight to giving the key scholarship tips!

With the aid of this book, aspirants can have a full view of suitable universities/colleges they can apply to and gain financial aid.

Here are Key Guidelines/Tips to Aid Students Win Scholarships

- **Apply By Early Action**: Students are advised to apply early in order to be duly considered for scholarship awards. The scholarship application for some schools goes together with the application for admissions, while other scholarship programs require entirely separate applications for them. Be sure to apply well ahead of the scholarship deadline(s).
  Note: Confirm the deadline of the scholarship and make sure you beat the deadline. Applications submitted after deadlines are usually disregarded.

- **Fill & Submit FAFSA**: Fill out and submit your FAFSA before the deadline. Filing a FAFSA is a requirement for many full ride scholarships. You'll learn more on the key definitions page of this book.

- **Apply For Scholarships You are Most Qualified For:** Scholarships have their requirements, these are put in place to provide the awards to deserving students. Therefore, it is highly advisable that you apply only for scholarships that you meet their requirements. It is also worth noting that meeting the minimum requirements doesn't guarantee that you'll obtain the scholarship. Why? Scholarships are competitive you should present yourself in the best way possible – by exuding excellence – to stand a chance. Scholarship opportunities at less known/less populated schools have shown to be easier to get.

- **Have a Good Test Score & GPA | Unique Talent**: SATs, ACTs, CLTs, and other grading system test scores should have been taken and scores obtained before applying for scholarships. A high test score combined with a superb high school GPA will increase the chances of you getting a scholarship as the majority of full ride scholarships are centered around the academic performance of scholars. Other criteria like leadership abilities, cultural background, unique talent, or life challenges are considered for some scholarships.

SCHOLARSHIP APPLICATION GUIDELINES

- **Craft Your Applications/ Essays to Impress:** Pay close attention to application essay topics and do thorough work in crafting a well-written essay and write to impress the reviewer highlighting your achievements in a very impressive manner. Ensure that your essay is well structured and free of any errors. Write award-winning essays!

- **Apply for as Many Scholarships as Possible:** Do not limit yourself to one scholarship. In as much as you meet the requirements for scholarships, give it your best shot. Several students have received multiple full ride scholarship offers from which they chose the best – that can be your story too.

- **Get Outstanding Recommendations/Nominations**: For scholarships requiring Nominations please ensure that you're nominated on time. Also, ensure that your recommendation letters show how much of an outstanding student you are.

- **Prepare Properly for Scholarship Interviews:** If the scholarship you apply for requires you to go through an interview process, prepare properly for it. Take your interview session with confidence.

- **DO NOT FALL Victim for Scholarship Scams.** Apply directly to the University/College of your interest or on the *official website* of the external scholarship(s) you wish to apply for. Do not enrich fraudsters using unauthorized means in applying for scholarships.

A Typical Scholarship Award Process

Find Scholarship(s) ➡ Start Application ➡ Submit Documents ➡

Submit Application ➡ Attend Interview (*Not applicable in all cases*)

⬇

$ Receive Scholarship/Get Feedback

✉ **Contact Us Here: https://bit.ly/chrisnuel-publishing**

Definition of Key Terms

What is FAFSA?

FAFSA stands for Free Application for Federal Student Aid.

To apply for federal student aid, such as federal grants, work-study, and loans, you need to complete the Free Application for Federal Student Aid (**FAFSA**®).

Some scholarship awards listed in this book require you to complete a FAFSA and to file it every year in order to get a renewal. Completing the FAFSA is not so much of a hassle — it is quite straightforward.

You can learn more about the FAFSA here; https://studentaid.gov/help/fafsa

A recommended FAFSA resource is "FAFSA Guru" on YouTube.

Who is a National Merit Scholar?

Started in 1955, the National Merit Scholarship Program is an academic scholarship competition for recognition and university scholarships, which is administered and managed by the National Merit Scholarship Corporation (NMSC). The NMSC is a privately funded, not-for-profit organization based in Evanston, Illinois.

Approximately 1.5 million high school students enter the program each year. Students are required to take the PSAT/NMSQT® and undergo some other evaluation process to be chosen as finalists.

Students who are chosen as semifinalists and finalist(s) may be eligible for some financial awards and recognitions.

The goal, however, should be for students to be selected as finalists (National Merit Scholars). National merit scholars receive special recognition and have access to National Merit® $2500 Scholarships, Corporate-sponsored Merit Scholarship awards, and College-sponsored Merit Scholarship awards.

College-sponsored scholarships in most cases can be up to full-ride or full-tuition scholarships.

Definition of Key Terms

What is PSAT/NMSQT?

The PSAT/NMSQT stands for Preliminary SAT/National Merit Scholarship Qualifying Test. PSAT/NMSQT is a standardized test administered by the College Board and co-sponsored by the National Merit Scholarship Corporation (NMSC). It is taken by millions of students each year.

The test scores from the PSAT/NMSQT are used to selected National Merit Scholars.

What are Test Scores?

Standardized tests are administered in the US each year for college admissions and other academic related activities. The college standardized tests in the US are:

- SAT
- ACT
- CLT (Accepted by a few schools)

High scores on these standardized tests (coupled with a high GPA) will give students a better chance of securing a full ride scholarship.

What to Expect in Future Editions of "The Full Ride Scholarship Book"?

In a nutshell, you should expect more amazing scholarship opportunities.

The next editions of this book will be updated with the latest full ride scholarships available in the U.S. — from institutional to external/private, and even the most hidden.

✉ **Contact Us Here: https://bit.ly/chrisnuel-publishing**

Other Scholarship Titles

The Full Tuition Scholarships Book: Pay Very Little for College

⌘ **Link to Book:**

https://www.amazon.com/s?k=The+full+tuition+scholarships+book

⌘ **ENJOY YOUR SCHOLARSHIPS !!!**

Notes

Made in the USA
Middletown, DE
05 May 2023